Professional Writing Skills
for Social Workers

SOCIAL WORK SKILLS IN PRACTICE

Series Editors:
Ruben Martin, Honorary Senior Lecturer in Social Work, University of Kent
Alisoun Milne, Professor of Social Gerontology and Social Work, University of Kent

Professional Writing Skills for Social Workers

Louise Frith and Ruben Martin

Open University Press

Open University Press
McGraw Hill
8th Floor, 338 Euston Road
London
England
NW1 3BH

email: enquiries@openup.co.uk
world wide web: www.openup.co.uk

First edition published 2015

A catalogue record of this book is available from the British Library

ISBN-13: 9780335249855
ISBN-10: 033524985X
eISBN: 9780335249862

Library of Congress Cataloging-in-Publication Data
CIP data applied for

Typeset by Transforma Pvt. Ltd., Chennai, India

Praise Page

"Communication, including writing skills, is an essential aspect of effective social work practice. Taking a practical and reflective approach, this text covers the foundations of professional writing in social work from the specific technical elements of writing, to writing professional reports and funding applications. The activities and reflective exercises included throughout the text provide opportunities to practice applying the skills to real-life-like situations. Writing matters, and this text serves as a useful resource to engage in and master effective writing skills for social work students all the way to seasoned social work practitioners."
—Barbra Teater, Professor of Social Work, College of Staten Island, City University of New York

"I wish I had had this book earlier in my career! Writing is an essential part of social work: for accountability (case notes), for decision making (writing helps us organise our thoughts) and for advocacy (writing is essential in arguing any case). Frith and Martin take us through the practical steps to improve our writing skills as practitioners and managers. This is not a book to read once and then put on the shelf but one to return to again and again. I will certainly be using my copy!"
—Luke Geoghegan, Head of Policy and Research, British Association of Social Workers

Contents

About the authors   *viii*

About the editors   *ix*

Series editor's foreword   *x*

Acknowledgements   *xi*

Part 1   Overview of professional writing   1

  1   Introduction   3
  2   Planning and organizing your writing   18
  3   Professional writing   33
  4   Technical aspects of writing   48

Part 2   Applying professional writing to social work practice   63

  5   Critical analysis in professional writing   65
  6   Correspondence   79
  7   Records   95
  8   Reports   112
  9   Funding applications   126
 10   Conclusion and continuing professional development   137

Appendix   *145*

References   *155*

Index   *158*

About the authors

Louise Frith is a Student Learning Adviser at the University of Kent where she teaches academic writing and study skills to students working in different disciplines across the university. She works closely with staff and students from the Social Work programme at the University of Kent to embed academic skills into the curriculum and prepare students for professional practice. Louise regularly contributes to the *Journal of Learning Development in Higher Education*, is a senior fellow of the Higher Education Academy and is on the National Advisory Board for the Academic Peer Learning Network.

Ruben Martin is Honorary Senior Lecturer in Social Work at the University of Kent, where he was Director of Studies for the BA (Hons) Social Work programme for seven years. He has been a probation officer and national training officer for a voluntary organization. Since his retirement from his full-time academic post in 2010 he has continued to work as a part-time lecturer and tutor, consultant, freelance practice educator, writer and editor. He is co-editor, alongside Alisoun Milne, of the Social Work Skills in Practice series from Open University Press & McGraw-Hill Education and author of another series title, *Teamworking Skills for Social Workers* (2013).

About the editors

The series is edited by Ruben Martin and Alisoun Milne.

Dr Alisoun Milne is Professor of Social Gerontology & Social Work at the University of Kent's School for Sociology, Social Policy and Social Research. She has managerial responsibilities for, and contributes to delivering, the University's undergraduate and postgraduate social work qualifying programmes. Alisoun is widely published in both academic and practice-related journals. Her key research interests are: social work with older people and their families; older carers; mental health in later life; and long-term care. Before becoming an academic in 1995 Alisoun worked as a social worker and team manager in two London boroughs. She is a member of the Association of Professors of Social Work, was on the Executive Committee of the British Society of Gerontology from 2009–15 and is a member of the Research Excellence Framework 2021 sub-panel for Social Work and Social Policy. She is registered with Social Work England.

Series editor's foreword

When Ruben Martin and I conceived of this series, our overriding ambition was to ensure that all books contained within it would have a clear and consistent focus on social work *skills*. Through our teaching, research and careers in practice, we had identified a need to better equip students and social work professionals with the competencies required to make a positive impact in service users' and carers' lives. Each book needs to be rigorous, clear and accessible; but above all, it has to be relevant and applied. From the outset, we felt that a book about professional writing skills was vital, given the significant impact that social workers' written words can have on the lives that they touch.

This is the second edition of 'Professional Writing Skills', revised and updated to take account of a number of key changes since the first edition was published in 2015. Changes include legislation relating to data protection, issues relating to digital communication, and new professional standards such as those developed by Social Work England - the regulator for social work education and practice in England since 2019.

Good writing skills are essential for good social work. It is a core skill required in a host of settings for a range of reasons. Being able to communicate effectively on paper and online, write a coherent cogent report, or present written evidence to a court will affect the lives of service users and their families, often in a profound and long term way. The writing skills explored in this book are not 'academic skills'. They are social work skills. Increasing emphasis on professionalism, ethics and values, the use of anti-oppressive language, and evidence-informed practice make this book essential reading for students, lecturers and practitioners alike. A newly qualified social worker will find the book invaluable.

Louise Frith and Ruben Martin skilfully carve an accessible, informed, and clear narrative through the ways in which writing skills are required, acquired and used in social work practice. The book is underpinned by professional skills and capabilities and by literature from educators and social work sources that informs, and explains, the different ways in which professional writing skills are deployed in social work practice. The book is infused with a commitment to high standards, articulating where writing skills are needed and how they make a difference; the authors helpfully distinguish between the different kinds of writing skills which different aspects of the social work role demand. The importance of writing as both a descriptive device and evidence of critical analysis is a real strength of the book, as is the argument that social workers need good writing skills to be able to do their jobs well - in all its various contexts and media and with different user groups and issues. The fusion of the authors' own skill sets and knowledge is writ large (excuse the pun...) in this book; at all times eloquent, readable, relevant, contemporary and future-facing. The book makes a powerful contribution to social work education and practice and provides a timely and rich source of knowledge, information, evidence and examples of professional writing skills for social workers.

Alisoun Milne

*Professor of Social Gerontology & Social Work, School for Sociology,
Social Policy and Social Research, University of Kent*

Acknowledgements

Our special thanks go to colleagues at the University of Kent Student Learning Advisory Service and Social Work staff group. Louise discussed chapters with Angela Koch and we both benefited from discussions with social work practitioners, including Alison Fullarton, Beth Payne and Alex Pringle. We would like to thank Open University Press and McGraw Hill Education editorial and production teams and in particular the invaluable help and support we have received from Open University Press commissioning editor Sam Crowe.

Part 1

Overview of professional writing

1 Introduction

As you start to read this, take a moment to consider the variety of writing that has some impact on you each day. All of us consume a huge amount of written material on a day-to-day basis, whether reading news headlines on an electronic tablet, smart phone or traditional newspaper, opening a letter from the bank, catching up on emails or glancing at adverts on public transport. We also read books, be it a novel, autobiography or a textbook like this one. As we regularly read such a variety of material, we may not notice or stop to consider whether what we are reading is well written and clear. We simply read, understand or process the information that the piece of writing has put forward for us.

However, there may well be instances when you have encountered some poor written English, which stands out and makes you wonder about the person or organization responsible for the writing. What would you think if you spotted a spelling or grammar mistake in a letter from your bank or your child's school? What if a friend asks you to check their CV and you notice that they have used some slang in it? Or perhaps you struggle through a complex sentence full of jargon in an academic textbook, which leaves you scratching your head. Think of the reaction you had to such writing and the effect it had on you as a reader. Did it amuse you, annoy or confuse you? Did you make assumptions about the person who wrote what you were reading? Did it change your opinion about the rest of that piece of writing? For example, did the bank or school's inaccuracies make you question whether the content of the letter was correct? You may have thought that your friend's CV made him or her sound unprofessional. Perhaps you thought that the author of a textbook had made the subject too academic and theoretical to be relevant to you as a future social work practitioner, so you switched off.

This book sets out to persuade you that writing well matters. It matters in all walks of life, but in a profession such as social work it matters for a number of particular reasons, which we go on to outline in this chapter. The purpose of this book is to help you to ensure that what you write as a social worker is appropriate to its audience and context, is ethical, professional, clear and unambiguous.

Why does writing well matter?

In a discussion about the basic foundations of education and how relevant they are to modern everyday life, Olah (2010: 1) refers to the initial idea of the 'three Rs':

> Back in the 1800s, Sir William Curtis, an alderman later dubbed Lord Mayor of London, made a toast to the Board of Education . . . about 'reading, 'riting and

'rithmetic' . . . It is unknown if he pronounced the words inaccurately on purpose due to illiteracy or if he was trying to be ironic. Either way, the phrase
was found intriguing and used by others.

It is still generally accepted that, together with the ability to read and the capacity to undertake numerical operations, proficiency in writing is a fundamental
part of what makes us educated human beings. If we go further back in history, in
ancient times the three 'lower arts' believed to be necessary for basic education
were grammar, logic and rhetoric. These three formed a *trivium* necessary as a
foundation before proceeding to higher education. Interestingly the modern word
trivia has acquired a broader, vaguer meaning relating to inconsequential general
knowledge. Grammar (structural rules of language), logic (putting forward a reasoned argument) and rhetoric (using language effectively and persuasively) will
feature in this book as these disciplines apply to professional writing.

Writing, as well as reading, is an activity that most of us undertake daily in
some form. We make notes to remind ourselves of what we have to do and to
remember information; we compile shopping lists and complete forms when we
are undertaking everyday transactions or major negotiations. We write to relatives and friends probably more through electronic means these days than by
sending traditional letters. We apply in writing for jobs and most types of employment involve some work-related writing.

A written job application is usually the first impression that you make to a prospective employer. The employer makes a judgement about you based on your
writing. A university careers adviser pointed out that the most common reason
cited by leading graduate employers to reject an application is English language
mistakes and poor spelling. If you hold a professional occupation you are expected
to write to a high standard. However, we may not always fully consider the com-
plexity of skills involved in writing.

Writing skills in social work

A national entry requirement to undertake a social work degree in the UK has for
some time been that candidates have at least a grade C in both maths and English
GCSC or their equivalent. This is a very basic prerequisite and compares unfa-
vourably with professions such as medicine and law, which traditionally have
entailed more years of education and training than social work. A low standard
of writing by social workers can give other professionals a poor impression and
undermine the authority and professional voice of social workers in general.

Beyond that basic requirement, entry standards vary among universities and
the calibre of social work students has been a subject of debate for some time. In
a report on the initial education of children's social workers commissioned by the
Secretary of State for Education, Sir Martin Narey (2014: 14) recounts that an
academic '. . . at one of the UK's top universities, told me that some social workers
graduating from some other institutions were barely literate'. While this statement
is vague and anecdotal, there is no reason to believe that Sir Martin was not can-
didly reporting a perception held by various social work educators or individuals

within the profession. Of course, this being an anecdote, we are not suggesting that all students in social work struggle to express themselves in written English.

The point of the above comments is to emphasize the importance of and need for a high level of professional writing in social work. We would not want at this stage to appear to be recommending this book to you only if you struggle with basic writing skills. Nevertheless, as you progress through your social work education and training, become a qualified social worker and develop professionally, we hope you will agree that it is helpful to review the requirements and standards of professional social work writing and the skills needed to achieve the necessary level. The chapters' content and sequence are summarized later in this introduction. We hope you will relate to the material where it confirms features of professional writing competence at which you are already proficient, but that you will also find that aspects of the book challenge you to reflect upon your own writing ability, and improve your existing skills.

Social work and paperwork

In 2016, Unison and Community Care produced a paper *A day in the life of social work*. The researchers 'asked more than 2,000 social work professionals to describe their day on 21 September 2016 to get a snapshot in time of the lives of social workers' (Unison, 2016). The report analyses responses and compares them with a similar survey carried out in 2014.

Case recording featured in 85% of responses, while 75% of respondents mentioned administration tasks and 58% report writing. This compares with 55% of respondents who said they had paid a visit to someone's house and 42% who reported having contact with a service user, child or family in an institutional setting (Unison, 2016).

This was very similar to the 2014 results. Reflecting on the day:

> Even after downing tools, 47% of workers said they'd finished their day with serious concerns about their cases. Despite many having worked above and beyond their contracted hours, almost three-quarters (74%) said this was because they'd been unable to get all the necessary paperwork finished.
>
> (Unison, 2016)

These findings are likely to resonate with many social workers. Social work practitioners spend a good deal of their time sitting at their computers writing. Keeping on top of this aspect of their workload can lead to anxiety. Paperwork is sometimes viewed by social workers as a distraction from 'real' social work. Many practitioners prefer to be interacting with service users rather than sitting at their computer. The volume of writing that social workers are required to manage is a matter for ongoing debate. In a speech to the National Children and Adult Services 2014 conference, Annie Hudson, chief executive officer of The College of Social Work (an organization that has since ceased to function), referred to overworked social workers being distracted by 'bureaucratic burdens'. Her views were reported in the national press with the headline, 'Social workers "need more secretaries and less paperwork'" (Dugan, 2014). Ms Hudson stated: 'Everyone recognizes we need to get social workers back to doing what they're good at' by freeing them up 'to do the work that they're qualified to do'.

There is bureaucracy in social work, and if it hinders effective professional practice it is damaging to the profession. It is right to want to avoid unnecessary paperwork. However, this book will argue that social workers should be 'good at' essential professional writing, which they should be 'qualified to do' to the required professional level. The 'real job' of a social worker *includes* paperwork. Social work starts with writing, and writing is an essential part of it. As a social worker you must be able to communicate effectively in writing with service users and fellow professionals. You must be able to keep records and write reports to a high standard. There will be other crucial writing such as that involved in seeking funding to benefit service users. This book aims to challenge the view that all paperwork is drudgery by giving you practical guidance and advice on how to write accurately and analytically. Professional writing requires thoughts to be ordered and evidence gathered, which can bring clarity to a complex situation; these skills can be developed with practice and feedback.

Professional capability

Social work reviews over the years have focused on ways of enhancing practice. The 2011 Munro Review of Child Protection addressed valuing and developing professional social work expertise in ways that apply not just to work with children and families but also to all service user groups. Sir Martin Narey (2014), mentioned above, was commissioned by the Department for Education to prepare a report on improving the education of social workers in children's services. Professor Croisdale-Appleby (2014) was commissioned by the Department of Health to undertake an independent review of social work education applicable to adult services. He suggested ways of improving the ability to provide all social workers with the right knowledge, skills and values.

Communicating in writing is a highly valued skill; now more than ever, social workers are required to improve their standards of writing so that they can communicate effectively with multiple audiences. Cafcass, for example, give good writing priority and suggest a clear structure in guidelines for their reports. These include 'co-production with the person concerned, so they are not misinterpreted'; 'No padding; nothing that is not to the point'; 'The woollier the writing, the longer the report and the harder it is to follow' (Douglas, 2017).

The Social Work Reform Board (SWRB, 2012), following the recommendations of a Social Work Task Force, proposed a professional capabilities framework (PCF) now administered by the British Association of Social Workers (BASW, 2018). It is a holistic concept with nine interdependent domains or areas of practice. It includes descriptions of capabilities outlining how practitioners are expected to evidence each domain at different levels of a student and social worker career. Although the PCF applies to social work in England, it dovetails with other frameworks and could be said to apply to social workers universally.

PCF domains

The *professionalism* domain is a reminder that all your writing should uphold the reputation of the profession and that your professional presentation should include reliability, honesty and respect. You must manage your time and workload, which includes paperwork, and recognize and maintain personal and professional boundaries. Your private opinions and biases should have no place in professional recording.

The social work profession's ethical principles and legislation need to be applied to writing as well as to other aspects of practice. The *values and ethics* domain suggests social workers should recognize the impact of their own values and demonstrate respectful partnership work with service users. It would be appropriate for you to record and report on how you are pursuing this and how you are promoting individuals' rights to autonomy and self-determination. Writing should be undertaken in a way that protects the privacy of individuals, recognizing the requirements of professional accountability and information-sharing.

The *diversity* domain is a reminder that the personal information you record can be based on an understanding of how an individual's identity is informed by factors such as culture, economic status, family composition, life experiences and characteristics. This domain requires you to recognize personal and organizational discrimination and oppression, and to question assumptions.

Where required, this book refers to appropriate legislation that highlights the need for you to work within the principles of human and civil rights and equalities as outlined in the *rights, justice and economic wellbeing* domain. Below is a reminder of some relevant legislation and its significance to professional social work writing.

Unlike academic writing, most professional writing in social work is more likely to reflect rather than to explicitly mention theoretical ideas included in the *knowledge* domain. Recording may help you understand aspects of human growth and development throughout the life course of service users. Reports may refer to the impact of psychological, socioeconomic, environmental and physiological factors in people's lives and forms of harm that impact on them. The centrality of relationships for people can be reflected in records of contact and involvement. All your writing should demonstrate that you value and take account of the expertise of service users, carers and professionals.

Professional writing will include and help you demonstrate *critical reflection and analysis*. It involves identification and gathering of information, rigorously questioning and evaluating the reliability and validity of information, and logical, systematic, critical and reflective reasoning. This domain requires you to formulate, test, evaluate and review hypotheses in response to information available and to formulate and make explicit evidence-informed judgements and justifiable decisions.

Within the *intervention and skills* domain there is a requirement that social workers must demonstrate capability to 'maintain accurate, comprehensible, succinct and timely records and reports ...' (BASW, 2018). However, as already stated, the focus of the framework is on holistic capabilities and interdependent domains, so the inclusion of report writing and record-keeping in this area should be taken into consideration within the context of all domains.

Writing is part of your working environment and the requirements of social workers explored in the *contexts and organizations* domain. You must understand lines of accountability and legal obligations. You must take responsibility for your role and impact within your work team, and be able to contribute positively to effective team working. Failing to note information and concerns in writing and not keeping on top of your paperwork has an impact on colleagues and affects the whole team as well as being an indication of poor professional practice.

The *professional leadership* domain is a reminder that you can recognize and start to demonstrate this capability as a student, as a newly qualified and early career social worker, as well as when you build experience and move into more senior positions. Records, for instance, can help you participate in supervision and you may make written contributions to staff meetings in ways that can support the learning and development of others as well as your own.

You may agree therefore that all the PCF domains apply to written work in a holistic way and are a reminder that you should regard writing as an integral part of your capabilities as a professional social worker.

Knowledge and Skills Statements

In 2013, chief social workers were appointed for children and families at the Department for Education (DfE), and for adults at the Department of Health and Social Care (DHSC). They published Knowledge and Skills Statements (KSS) for children and family practitioners, and for social workers in adult services, respectively. To supplement the broader and more generic PCFs, KSS set out what a social worker should know and be able to do at the end of their Assessed and Supported Year in Employment.

KSS for children and family practitioners include:

Produce written case notes and reports, which are well argued, focused, and jargon free. Present a clear analysis and sound rationale for actions as well as any conclusions reached, so that all parties are well informed.

(DfE, 2018)

KSS for social workers in adult services include being able to:

... communicate clearly, sensitively and effectively, applying a range of best evidence-based methods of written, oral and non-verbal communication and adapt these methods to match the person's age, comprehension and culture. Social workers should be capable of communicating effectively with people with specific communication needs, including those with learning disabilities, dementia, people who lack mental capacity and people with sensory impairment.

(DoH, 2015)

Professional standards

Until 2012, the General Social Care Council (GSCC) was the national regulator, registering social workers and upholding social work's standards. These responsibilities were then taken on by the Health and Care Professions Council (HCPC), a body that already regulated other health professions. However, in 2018 Social Work England (SWE) was established and since December 2019 it has become the regulator for social work, working in tandem with comparable bodies in other UK countries.

In 2019, SWE published professional standards setting out what a social worker must know, understand and be able to do. The expectation on social workers is that they will promote people's rights and wellbeing; establish and maintain the trust and confidence of people; be accountable for their practice; maintain continuous professional development; act safely and with integrity; and promote ethical practice.

SWE Professional Standards Guidance addresses communication and states that:

> Information should always be given in a form, language, and manner that people can understand. It is important that social workers reflect their considerations around communication in their records and review them appropriately. Social workers should consider whether technology-based communication tools can facilitate communication with people. It is important that social workers are familiar with emerging technologies and the appropriate ways of using technology to aid communication.
>
> (SWE, 2020)

Although the capabilities, knowledge, skills and standards outlined above apply specifically to England, they are based on skills, knowledge and values that would be expected from a social worker anywhere in the UK and indeed internationally. They are worth noting therefore even if you are a social worker practising under a different regulator in other countries of the UK or further afield.

Legislation

The Data Protection Act 2018 entitles service users and carers to access what is written about them upon request. It gives citizens the right to view data that organizations, both private and public bodies, hold about them. It largely maintains the provision of a previous Data Protection Act (1998). The 1998 Act was superseded by the 2018 Act to make data protection laws fit for increasingly digital forms of data processing and to ensure its requirements were in keeping with the European Union (EU) General Data Protection Regulation (GDPR) standards. The 2018 Act aims to protect freedoms, particularly the privacy of individuals. It ensures data that can be used to identify an individual is not processed without their knowledge and that it is used fairly and legally with their consent wherever possible. This applies to data held electronically and manually.

A professional who records and stores personal data concerning service users in order to work with them is responsible for that data. Service users may make a request to view data concerning them, as the Act gives them the right to see all information that is held about them. In addition to data in files, service users may request access to any unstructured information that may be within emails, correspondence, telephone messages, internal memos and contact records. Data can only be withheld if disclosure would be likely to cause serious harm to the service user or any other person's physical or mental health. A request for information will take into account the age and capacity of the individual making it.

In May 2018, GDPR came into force, the regulations having been previously agreed by the European Parliament and Council. They state that anyone who has given information to a company or organization has to give permission for it to be kept and used. Anything that could be deemed as misusing or mishandling data can have severe consequences. An example of this is a social worker who was sanctioned with a one-year 'conditions of practice order' by the then regulator, HCPC, for forwarding confidential service user information to a personal email address. This was reported in *Community Care* (Stevenson, 2017). GDPR is underpinned by seven principles:

1. *Lawfulness, fairness and transparency.* When data is kept by an organization, it must be clear why it is doing so and how the data is going to be used. A data subject, including social work service users, may request further information about the data and to see what has been written about them under a Subject Access Request (SAR) provision.
2. *Purpose limitation.* Organizations can only use personal information data for a specific, legitimate purpose.
3. *Data adequacy and minimization.* Organizations must only store the minimum amount of data required for the stated purpose. They must not add to it in case it might be useful in future.
4. *Accuracy.* Personal data must be correct, fit for purpose and current. An individual may request that factually wrong data be corrected and a person may require that data is not used in any way that may cause damage or distress.
5. *Storage limitation.* Data must be deleted or destroyed once it is no longer needed.
6. *Meeting the individual's rights.* People have the right to access personal data and stop it being misused. Individuals can request to see information held about them by submitting a SAR.
7. *Integrity and confidentiality.* Organizations must ensure that data is safe and secure and protected from unauthorized use.
8. *Accountability.* Organizations must be responsible for complying with the regulations. This includes appointing a designated data protection officer.

GDPR is enforced by the Information Commissioner's Office (ICO) and the Government has confirmed that the UK's decision to leave the European Union (EU) as a result of the 2016 referendum would not alter this. Although this decision resulted in some uncertainty about the status of EU regulations, there was no change from the time of the UK formally leaving the EU on 31 January 2020 to the end of a transition period up to 31 December 2020. The UK Government has issued a statutory instrument amending the Data Protection Act 2018 and merging it with the requirements of the EU GDPR. This new regime will be known as the 'UK GDPR'.

Other than an individual's request concerning their own personal data under a SAR, all requests for information received by a public body are required to be answered in accordance with the Freedom of Information Act 2000 or the Environmental Information Regulations 2004. They give any person the right to make a request for information held by a public authority. The requirements do not apply to private bodies. The main principles include everyone's right to know about the activities of public sector organizations. The provisions give members of the public the right to request and access official information, which may be in files, emails, minutes of meetings, records and reports. In addition to members of the public, the Freedom of Information Act and Environmental Information Regulations can be used by journalists, researchers and others who may be legitimately seeking to ask any public authority for the recorded information it has on any subject. If a service user or carer asks for information a public organization holds about them, the request will be handled under the Data Protection Act.

The European Convention on Human Rights (ECHR) was enshrined in UK legislation through the Human Rights Act 1998. It is unlawful for a public body to act in a way that is incompatible with human rights in the Convention. These include the right for citizens to experience no discrimination and to be treated fairly in respect of gender, race, sexual orientation, religion or age. The Act upholds the right to a fair hearing and to a private and family life, protecting individuals against unnecessary surveillance or intrusion into their lives. If a service user or carer can show that a public authority has interfered with a right outlined in the Act, they may take action by contacting the organization to remind them of their obligations or by taking the matter to court. Social work records and any other written information should be kept and maintained in accordance with these rights.

The intention in this book is not to provide you with a legal manual. Its focus is on professional writing skills, rather than official procedures and protocols. Nevertheless, the legislation mentioned above, which is in keeping with professional social work values, has implications for writing reports and keeping records. Key points to remember include:

- recording personal information about service users and carers may seem intrusive, so what you include must at all times be necessary and fit for purpose;
- when writing you should bear in mind that service users and carers may read what you have recorded about them;
- all forms of writing about service users and carers must be respectful, relevant, accurate, up to date and dated, so that anyone reading it subsequently will know when the information was recorded;
- you should take your responsibility to maintain records and reports seriously;
- your writing must be professional and ethical, not only in official reports but also in emails and more informal means of communication as well.

Who is this book for?

The content of this book, summarized in the 'Book structure' section below, will be of interest and use to social workers at all levels but especially those who are at an early stage in their careers. If you are a qualified practitioner, the book may provide you with challenge, guidance, suggestions to improve your writing and to make it more professional; you may also find confirmation of your strengths and capabilities. If you are a newly qualified social worker (NQSW) in the UK, you will be subject to extra requirements and support to pursue your professional development. These include programmes such as an Assessed Year in Employment (AYE) in Northern Ireland; a Consolidation Programme in Wales; and Post Registration Training and Learning (PRTL) in Scotland. In England, NQSWs follow an Assessed and Supported Year in Employment (ASYE) that requires the compiling of a portfolio with practice-based evidence of meeting KSS. The portfolio will include professional documentation such as examples of professional writing that you have undertaken as part of your work. Reflective writing is generally required for NQSW portfolios and as evidence of pursuing your continuing professional development (CPD) record.

The book will also be of interest and help to you if you are a social work student, particularly in your practice placements, as you start tackling aspects of professional writing expected from and required by social care organizations and social work agencies. Professional writing skills are crucial for all social work students, but there are aspects of this book that may be specifically helpful to you if you come from a different education system to that in the UK, or if English is not your first language.

The book is applicable to practitioners in other professions as well, especially those who work in a multidisciplinary way and inter-professionally with social workers.

Aims and approach

Writing a book about writing is a risky activity. We trust that this book will demonstrate the essence of what is outlined within it, such as the organization of writing, a formal style, appropriate tone and adherence to required technical aspects of writing. One aim has been to make the book clear and coherent and we hope that you will forgive lapses where we could have more precisely put into practice what we suggest to readers. In writing this book we assume that you as a reader have a basic capability in written communication but that you want to explore and review your professional writing skills. Our aims include the expectation that the book will help you:

- understand the importance of professional writing;
- differentiate professional writing from other forms such as personal and academic writing;
- see writing in social work as a way of demonstrating professionalism;
- integrate writing as part of your social work practice;
- enhance your capability to write analytically;
- locate writing as an aid to decision-making in social work;
- accept the need to appropriately address differing audiences in your professional writing.

Book structure

The book is divided into two parts. Part 1, an overview of professional writing, focuses on planning and organizing your writing, on writing in a professional style and on technical aspects of good English writing. Part 2 applies professional writing to social work practice and reviews the types of writing that social workers undertake.

In Part 1, this introduction (Chapter 1) explores the need for professional writing in social work and the importance of it for effective work with service users and colleagues within social work and in multidisciplinary settings. Chapter 2 gives suggestions for preparing to write. It highlights differences between academic and professional writing and stresses the need to keep in mind who the writing is for – different audiences, work settings and sectors. It gives suggestions for planning, different approaches to, and structuring, writing. Chapter 3 explores what is involved in a professional style of writing. It includes looking at ways in which language can be objective and formal and how writing can be analytical. It reviews a professional vocabulary. Chapter 4, addressing technical aspects of writing, highlights the need to be conversant with correct grammar, punctuation and spelling; for writing to be cohesive, clear and coherent; and ways of keeping language simple and elegant rather than complex.

Introducing Part 2, Chapter 5 explores critical analysis in professional writing, applying this to the increasingly varied context of social work practice that is emerging. It includes a comparison of descriptive and analytical writing, a discussion of how to convey a professional voice, and the role that social workers play to negotiate and facilitate outcomes in writing on behalf of service users. Chapter 6 discusses the style and appropriateness of various forms of communication that social workers use to correspond with other professionals and with service users, including emails, letters, memos, text messages and online media profiles. Chapter 7 looks at practical ways for social workers to keep a record of their work in clear, succinct and comprehensive ways, appropriate for purpose. The chapter reviews various types of notes, records, plans, chronologies and minutes. Chapter 8 addresses the requirements of writing reports, their structure and expectations. It suggests ways of planning a report, and including within it necessary sections to help the reader. Chapter 9 explores aspects of writing funding applications to internal panels, external charities and trusts, and seeking funding for projects and research. The final chapter, 10, summarizes many of the themes outlined earlier and stresses the importance of writing for one's own CPD and professional identity.

Interacting with the book

The book structure follows a logical sequence, so it is useful to have covered material in earlier chapters as you move on to later ones, particularly in Part 1. However, we appreciate that textbooks are not necessarily intended to be read from cover to cover as you might a novel. Do not feel guilty if you go directly to an individual chapter, or a section of it, because the content interests you or if you have found something that you believe will be of particular help to you. So do look through the list of chapters, the index, this introduction, headings and so on, to focus on the areas that you might find most useful.

Each chapter starts with an overview and an introduction and ends with a summary, conclusion and key points from the chapter. As you read through you will find additional features that will help you interact with the material. There are reflection points to encourage you to stop and think about your practice and issues related to the content at that point, thus applying these to your experience. It is a good idea to write down your reflections for future reference. Other stopping points involve exercises and activities to help you consider and delve into aspects of the topic being explored. The book also includes examples of writing from practice to enable you to see how what is being discussed applies to the real world of work. At the end of each chapter there are suggestions for further reading and other sources that will enable you to pursue topics further.

Limitations

This is a book about professional writing skills for social workers but it is unlikely that your skills will develop merely through reading it, even if you persevere through all the chapters. Interacting with the book in ways suggested above will take you a step further. In addition, you will need to practise skills in ways suggested by the book and seek feedback on your writing. At the end of this chapter there is an individual checklist of writing skills. It is intended for you to assess your skills level and review it as you delve into sections of the book that expand on particular skills. We would also recommend that you read further and research other sources, including online ones. There is also a lot that can be learned from colleagues' feedback and from reading the writing of more experienced co-workers. Throughout your career, but especially in the early stages, it is vital that you are open to and accept feedback and even criticism of your writing in order to improve. Even the most experienced practitioners say that communication, whether in written or spoken form, is a skill area which they must continuously review and improve throughout their career.

The book addresses professional writing skills in social work generally as they apply to different service user groups, settings and sectors. Different organizations, local authorities and teams dealing with specific work develop their own documentation, systems, protocols, policies and procedures. This book cannot provide you with the detailed training that your employer should offer you during induction, your ASYE and in CPD initiatives. The examples in this book are typical ones from practice but may not be in the exact format used by your agency. Nevertheless, you can take a good deal of initiative to apply what is in this book to your specific practice and take responsibility for your own learning and development.

Writing skills checklist

Below is a list of skills relating to professional writing in social work reviewed in this book. You may find it helpful to score yourself against each one before and after reading the book. You can look up appropriate sections where the book explores what is involved in developing these skills, particularly the ones for which you give yourself a low score.

Skill	Score from 1–5 1 = I need to develop this skill 5 = I am proficient at this skill	See page(s)
Addressing requirements of professional, rather than academic, writing		20–21
Having a clear objective or purpose for every writing task		22
Planning and making time to write		23
Gathering information		23
Using mind maps or other planning tools		23–24
Assessing your audience		24
Adjusting your writing to specific audiences		24
Keeping sentences short		24
Using active verbs and sentences		25
Knowing when it is appropriate to use passive sentences		25
Using first or third person appropriately		25–26
Using words that are appropriate for the reader		26
Giving instructions within your writing		27
Avoiding abstract nouns		28
Using lists when appropriate in your writing		28
Structuring paragraphs		29
Inserting key sentences		29
Using signposting language		29
Using conjunctions		30
Using subheadings		30
Writing in a professional style		33–34
Adjusting your writing style (formal/informal) as appropriate		34
Avoiding repetition and redundancy		35
Using a professional vocabulary		35
Being clear about the meaning and spelling of words		35–37
Writing instructions to someone		38
Describing a process		38
Writing persuasively		39

$\longrightarrow$

(continued)

Skill	Score from 1–5 **1 = I need to develop this skill** **5 = I am proficient at this skill**	See page(s)
Summarizing using a limited number of words		40
Using words and phrases that indicate analysis		41
Writing in an appropriate tone		42
Using non-discriminatory and non-oppressive language		42
Using correct verb tenses		48
Using more than one verb tense correctly within a sentence or paragraph		50
Ensuring the verb is in agreement with the subject in your sentences		52
Using noun phrases		53
The correct use of: commas		54–55
semicolons and colons		55–56
apostrophes		57–58
contractions		57
Adding qualifying statements		59
Adding examples to strengthen your writing		60
Gathering relevant evidence to include in reports		68–69
Checking for bias in your writing and others' writing		70–71
Expressing your professional voice in writing		74
Identifying weaknesses in your writing and in others' writing		75–76
Making recommendations which are realistic		76–77
Writing professional correspondence: emails		81–83
letters		83–85
later life letters		86
memos		86–87
text messages		88–89
online social media profiles		90–93

$\longrightarrow$

(continued)

Skill	Score from 1–5 1 = I need to develop this skill 5 = I am proficient at this skill	See page(s)
Writing professional records: case records or case notes		105
contact or running records		106
day and residential work records		106
care plans		107
action plans		107
support plans		108
chronologies		108–109
minutes		110
Using paragraphs and headings to structure reports		114
Making effective use of free text boxes		67, 73
Familiarity with the different types of report your agency uses		118–122
Identifying and describing impact		117, 124
Identifying the reasons why things happen as they do		112, 117
Interpreting charts, diagrams and data		116
Writing funding applications: within your agency		127–130
from external sources (charities, trusts)		130–132
for projects and other proposals		133–135
Understanding the importance of writing for your own CPD and professional identity		142–144

Further reading

Rai, L. (2014) *Effective Writing for Social Work: Making a Difference*, Bristol: Policy Press.
Williams, P. (2018) *Advanced Writing Skills for Students of English*, English Lessons Brighton, an imprint of Rumian Publishing.

2 Planning and organizing your writing

Chapter overview

By the end of this chapter you should have an understanding of:

- a variety of approaches to writing and the differences between academic and professional writing;
- the skills involved in gathering information;
- the purposes of professional writing;
- the significance of knowing the audience for your professional writing;
- the principles of writing and structuring in concise language.

Introduction

Social workers' writing is a lasting record of their work. The PCF professionalism domain (BASW, 2018), referring to social workers, states that, 'As representatives of the social work profession, they safeguard its reputation and are accountable to the professional regulator'. This chapter outlines the steps involved in preparing to write as a professional. It considers the context and audiences for professional writing in social work and the difficulties that may arise when writing for very diverse groups of people, such as other professions (e.g. health professionals, teachers, legal professionals) and service users, including people for whom English is not their first language, people with dementia or people with learning disabilities. Various approaches to writing will be examined so that you can reflect on your own writing strategies. The chapter will suggest some ways to structure writing using key sentences, signposting, subheadings and paragraphing. You will be encouraged to reflect on your strengths in written communication. There are practice exercises throughout the chapter for you to test your skills as you progress.

Writing as part of thinking

Writing has long been recognized as an important mechanism in the thinking process; it allows professionals to reflect on their actions, plan the next steps and communicate this to others. It is useful, therefore, to block time in your day for writing and to ensure that this is valued by your supervisor. This can be done by sharing writing with your team and supervisor and using reports to stimulate team discussions or supervision meetings. As mentioned in the previous chapter, you may sometimes hear complaints that paperwork is taking social workers away from the 'real job' of being a social worker; however, it has always been a necessary part of being a professional. Much of the writing that you as a social worker will do is used as the basis for making important decisions for and with service users, or is shared with other professionals who are also working with the service user. The Munro Report (2011) highlighted the supreme importance of agencies sharing information; in order to do this, clear records need to be kept and accessed. The quality of your written work is read and often judged by other professionals, so it is important for your own professional credibility and the status of the profession in general that it is of high quality. Therefore, rather than resisting writing, you can view it positively as a way in which you can do the job of a social worker more effectively.

Approaches to writing

Although writing experts always advise planning before you write, there are different ways to do this (depending on your time, learning style and personality):

- **Activists** are inclined to jump straight in and start writing, allowing the words to take shape as they write. This process often involves a lot of editing and cutting, but it can work.
- **Reflectors** tend to read and think a lot before they write and then they are able to write in one sitting, with the shape of their writing in their head. This approach to writing often does not require much editing.
- **Adrenaline junkies** procrastinate for days and hours before writing and only seem to be able to get the words out when the deadline is absolutely on top of them. This can be a risky approach because writing can take more time than anticipated, so it may be useful to make interim deadlines and ask colleagues to help you to keep to them.
- **Scaffolders** are able to write a basic outline of their writing and then do the work to find out information which will fit into their outline.

Reflection

- What do you think are the advantages and disadvantages of these different approaches?
- To what extent do you recognize yourself in any of these types?

You may have recognized something problematic about your approach – for example, if you are an activist you may need to develop a scaffolding technique for writing complex reports, or you may find that the benefits of being reflective are lost if you then become overwhelmed with information. However, it is quite likely that you are able to recognize more than one approach to writing in yourself, or that for different writing tasks you take different approaches. This is an indication that you have a flexible approach to writing and you are able to adapt your approach depending on the task. This is ultimately what you will need to be able to do to be an effective professional.

How is writing for university different to writing in professional practice?

Developing a good writing style at university is of enormous benefit when you enter professional practice, because you will have practised writing to a word limit, which enhances your ability to write concisely. You will also have had experience of summarizing information and analysing it against a range of different theoretical approaches. University writing is, of course, like professional writing, done under the pressure of time and deadlines and it is therefore good practice for professional life. These days many students, especially social work students who may come to study later in life, are balancing study with work or family life. This is very difficult, but it does at least give students a taste for the stresses to come at work.

Although your university degree prepares you in many ways for professional practice, there are some key differences between the writing that you do as a student and that which you do as a social work practitioner.

Writing for university	Professional writing
At university the **audience** you write for is academic. When you write your essays and reports you have in mind your lecturers; this means that you assume certain knowledge and that you are aware of the way in which assignments are marked (with references to theory and analytical frameworks).	In professional writing the **audience** is much more varied; you may be writing for your manager or other colleagues in your team, but you may also be writing to inform other professionals such as police, teachers and health care professionals. Most importantly, you need to be aware that service users will also have access to everything that you write about them. This inevitably changes the way in which you write. You will at times be writing for and to service users.
The **purpose** of writing at university is first and foremost to demonstrate your learning and meet the learning outcomes of the module of study; therefore, this type of writing tends to be structured around theoretical knowledge.	Professional writing in social work has many different **purposes**; you may be writing up notes on a service user's progress, or a report for a court case, or drafting a care plan. These purposes for writing are very specific and have an impact on the lives of your service users.
In academic writing, **definitions** are important. It is often necessary to define terms early on in a piece of academic writing so that your marker knows exactly what you are arguing.	Professional writing also requires clarity of terms and it is even less easy to assume a shared understanding of this, so clear **definitions** are vital.

Writing for university	Professional writing
Academic **writing style** is highly formal. Students are usually encouraged to use objective language in the third person and to start sentences with noun forms (e.g. 'it might be interpreted that . . .') unless you are writing about your practice (e.g. a case study).	**Writing style** for professional practice must also be formal, but it is often more direct than academic writing. It can address the reader directly and it normally follows the subject–verb–object sequence in sentences (e.g. 'Ruben writes books').
To **structure** academic writing students are usually recommended to avoid lists and instead write in unbroken prose and passive structures.	In professional writing lists are often preferable to unbroken prose, because the main purpose of the writing is to get your message across as quickly and clearly as possible.
Academic writing puts strong emphasis on **referring to sources** of information and referencing.	Professional writing requires specific reference to evidence perhaps for arguing for more provision, but in most written communication academic referencing is not appropriate.
Academic writing is **assessed** and a pass mark (usually 40% or 50%) allows for some weaknesses in the use of English, structure and content.	Although professional writing is not formally assessed it is scrutinized by an audience, so what is good enough for a minimum academic pass mark is unlikely to be acceptable for professional writing within a social work agency.

Activity 2.1

The following extract is from a social work student's case study assignment from a placement.* The student was placed in a rehabilitation day centre for people with mild-to-moderate brain injury. In the extract, the student describes her preparation for meeting a new service user. Rewrite this information so that it may be read by other colleagues who may be working with X. Is there anything you would leave out, or give more prominence to and why?

At the initial meeting I aimed to identify X's needs and work in partnership with her to plan how those needs might be met. According to Hatton (2005), communication is a vital process in social work and 'lies at the heart of social work practice'. I asked open questions to explore and identify the issue of risk associated with the presenting problem by encouraging X to tell me what her husband is doing that poses a risk to her health. She told me that due to her husband's dementia, he had been displaying some inappropriate behaviour; he had left the house a couple of times without informing her, he got lost which involved the police bringing him back home. She also informed me that her husband escaped the residential home where he was on respite when she was on holiday at the Isle of Wight. This information led me to work with X, through the use of a 'genogram' in order to gain a holistic understanding of the relationships within her family (Wilson et al. 2008) and to also present issues that are difficult to verbalize in a pictorial form without interrogating as suggested by Meacham (2009). X revealed to me that her relationship with her husband was very poor due to his excessive drinking; she does not have much contact with her step-daughter but stressed good support from her son.

*Reader please note: the references in this activity are fictional, hence not listed in the reference section.

For suggested changes, see appendix, page 145.

In professional writing you do not need to make reference to literature or explain your methodology, but you must be clear and accurate.

The purposes of professional writing

Although the specific purposes of different social work writing tasks will be examined in more detail in later chapters, this section considers the overarching importance of having a clear objective for every writing task, no matter how small that task seems. For example, even an email needs to convey information, whether that is to describe events, provide facts, apologize, instruct, explain or provide a perspective to promote debate. All of your professional writing should have a logical sequence, a chronology of events, if appropriate, and should consist of facts and professional judgements rather than personal opinion.

Before embarking on a writing task you must be absolutely certain of the purpose. It may be necessary to discuss this with a colleague or supervisor so that you are sure. Knowing the purpose of a writing task helps you to make crucial decisions about what to include and leave out, and what language style you use, and it also helps to make your writing flow better. In short, your aim at this stage is not to know what to write, but to know what you want to achieve.

Example

Writing task	Objective
Email to school	To inform colleagues from other agencies of a change in a service user's circumstances
Initial assessment	To evaluate a service user's needs and make recommendations for other colleagues, both inside and outside of social work, to work towards supporting the service user
Case notes	To describe and provide facts about a case which may be used in future by other professionals or accessed by the service user
Court report	To evaluate a service user's character and behaviour, describe any changes in these and make recommendations to the court
Care plan	To identify how the needs of a service user will be met, highlight the priorities and outline a care package

Planning and making time to write

Although not many of us plan writing formally, we do all plan things in our heads. This is important in order to enable us to get writing done without undue stress. Writing, like anything else, needs to be practised if we are to become skilled at it, and there are usually certain times of the day when we can be more productive, especially if we find writing difficult. It is useful to try to analyse a working week, identify the times when you can write and try to ring-fence those times so that they are prioritized for the difficult writing tasks you have in a week. If this does not happen, you are likely to find yourself taking writing tasks home and doing them at inappropriate times such as evenings and weekends when you are not at your best and which may well result either in mistakes or in unhealthy levels of stress for yourself.

Gathering information

For any writing task you will need to gather relevant information. In social work this is about asking appropriate questions and allowing service users to give full answers. There is considerable literature elsewhere about communication skills such as neuro-linguistic programming (NLP), which seeks to address immediate emotional responses and educate people about self-awareness and effective communication; and discourse analysis, which aims at revealing the social and psychological characteristics of the person who is communicating rather than just a text analysis of the words they use. This book does not discuss these techniques, although they are of vital relevance to social workers. Gathering information is the start of the writing process, so it is important for social workers to keep accurate notes of all conversations they have with service users so that the information can be used to argue for resources or support for individuals.

Activity 2.2

Consider an older person who has had a fall at home in her bathroom and as a consequence has had a period in hospital. Your task is to investigate whether she needs access to services or support. What specific questions might you need to ask?

For suggested questions, see appendix, page 145.

Many writers find that putting this information into a 'mind map' can help them to see the issue more clearly and start to make links between things. A mind map is a way of capturing information in a diagram and can act as a useful visual tool for organizing your thoughts. Figure 2.1 is an example of a semi-complete mind map. Try to add more information to it.

As a result of gathering this type of information you should be in a much better position to set clear objectives for the way in which you write an assessment report and a possible care plan.

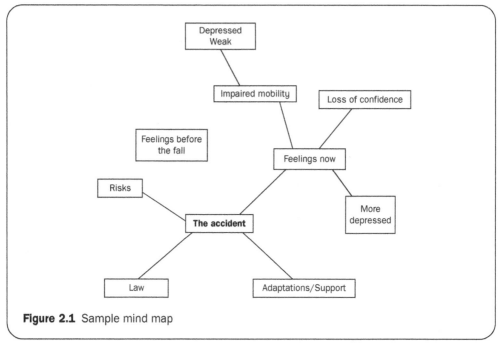

Figure 2.1 Sample mind map

Audiences: who are they and what do they need to know?

Although for most writing tasks you will be aware of the audience for your writing, sometimes you will have more than one audience or you may have a primary and a secondary audience. All records relating to a service user may be available for them to read on request, so it is important to bear this in mind whenever you write. There are three essential elements to assessing your audience:

1. Focus on the information they **need to know**.
2. **Explain terms** or concepts that may be confusing or complex.
3. **Predict** and address **questions** which they may have.

Readers of social workers' professional writing are very diverse. They range from legal professionals, teachers, police, doctors and other social workers to people with learning disabilities, young people, people with mental health problems and people for whom English is not their first language. The PCF (BASW, 2018) requires social workers to be aware of discrimination, which can be caused by language. For some service users, particularly adults, you may consider it appropriate sometimes to work with the service user to ensure that their voice is heard within writing which relates to them. Therefore, clarity and simplicity of expression are essential. The following section gives you guidance on how to do this.

Clarity and simplicity

Keep your sentences short

The average length of a sentence should be between approximately 15 and 20 words. This allows you to develop your points, but is not so long that the reader forgets the subject of the sentence. Each sentence must be complete and not dependent on its predecessor/successor for comprehension. Sometimes it is useful for you to read what you have written aloud so that you can hear mistakes or identify sentences that are incomplete.

Use active verbs

There are three main parts to every sentence; in active sentences the word order is as follows:

- a subject (the person, group or thing doing the action);
- a verb (the action itself);
- an object (the person, group or thing that the action is done *to*).

For example, 'She *(subject)* argued *(verb)* with her daughter *(object)*.' However, in passive sentences this is reversed so that the object comes first, then the verb and finally the subject. Compare these three examples of active and passive sentences. Passive sentences can be confusing, and often make the sentences longer and less lively.

> This case will be considered by me shortly.
> I will consider this case shortly.

> The violence was stopped by the police.
> The police stopped the violence.

> The home had to be closed by the local authority.
> The local authority had to close the home.

In general it is best to try to avoid using the passive form. However, there are some occasions where its use is appropriate. Here are some examples.

To make something sound less hostile:

> He did not attend the meeting.
> This meeting was not attended.

To avoid apportioning blame:

> We have made a mistake.
> A mistake has been made.

When you do not know who or what the 'doer' is:

> She made a decision regarding . . .
> A decision has been made regarding . . .

Generally, you should aim for about 80 to 90 per cent of your sentences to be active and only use passive sentences where necessary.

Use *you*, *we* and *I*

In academic writing the use of the first person pronoun (I/we/you) is discouraged; however, in professional writing for social work it is usually better to use first person pronouns as they are a more direct form of expression. This is especially useful when you are writing directly for a service user. In these situations it is much clearer to use *you* and *we* or *I*.

Example

> *Assessment of the case is deemed high priority: therefore it is advised that an appointment be made as soon as possible so that a comprehensive care plan can be discussed.*

> This could be unclear, as it does not contain a clear instruction to the reader.

Better

> *We have assessed you as 'high priority'; therefore, we would like you to come in for interview as soon as possible so that we can agree a comprehensive care plan.*

Use words that are appropriate for the reader

Generally this means using words that are familiar, but not necessarily simple words. It is also good practice to try to avoid using jargon, including acronyms which may only be understood by certain people. To do this, try to imagine that you are talking directly to your reader and use terms that do not need explanation. If technical language is unavoidable, then give a clear meaning or illustration immediately.

Activity 2.3

Look at the following common social work jargon. What else could you say instead of using the jargon?

Social work jargon	Suggested alternative
Carer's stress	
Community care	
Multi-agency approach	
Person-centred approach	
Respite care	
Service user empowerment	
Value-driven policy	

For suggested alternatives, see appendix, page 145.

It is also helpful to avoid the use of abbreviations. Local authorities use a system code for types of abuse, for instance, but referring only to the code, which can in any case change over the years, will mean your record holds little if any meaning to someone not familiar with the code.

Activity 2.4

Would you agree that it is best to avoid words and abbreviations such as those in the list below? Can you provide alternatives to them? Can you add to the list?

- CHIN
- Integrated care
- LCSB
- Ongoing
- Personalization
- Pre-assessment
- Psychosocial support
- Reablement
- Resource allocation system (RAS)
- Sect. 47
- Significant harm
- Wellbeing

For suggested alternatives, see appendix, page 146.

As well as avoiding jargon it is also helpful to write in plain English, avoiding complex language. Therefore, you need to consider carefully how you are going to phrase what you record.

Do not be afraid to give instructions

Although it is often considered impolite to make commands, this is often the most direct and simplest way to inform your audience of what is expected from them. If you are concerned that commands sound too harsh you can begin with *please*.

Please send it to me.
not
I should be grateful if you would send it to me.

Please respond in writing by the end of this month.
not
You are advised to respond in writing no later than the end of the month.

Avoid abstract nouns

Abstract nouns (things which are not physically present) are often formed from verbs, as the following examples show.

Verb	Abstract noun
to complete	completion
to introduce	introduction
to fail	failure
to provide	provision
to arrange	arrangement
to investigate	investigation
to discuss	discussion
to implement	implementation

We discussed the matter.
not
We had a discussion about the matter.

The team has implemented the recommendations.
not
Implementation of the recommendations has been carried out.

The problem with abstract nouns is that like passive sentences they sound as if nothing is really happening. They can be confusing and can also lead to a dull and bureaucratic writing style.

Use lists where appropriate

Bullet point lists are easy to read and encourage the reader to pay attention to each item on the list, whereas a list which is part of a sentence can be more diffi-cult to read. For example, a service user has been given the following advice, if she encounters a particular situation in the future, to remain calm, avoid engag-ing in conversation and write down all incidents however minor they may seem. This would be easier to read if it was in list form:

* remain calm;
* avoid engaging in conversation;
* write down all incidents however minor they may seem.

Activity 2.5

This extract is an explanation of the five principles of the Mental Capacity Act (2005). Rewrite this statement so that it addresses the service user directly and uses some of the principles outlined above.

The Mental Capacity Act 2005 contains five principles; the client has presumed capacity, the client has all the support they need to make a decision, if the client makes an unwise decision, this does not indicate they do not have the capacity to understand, if the client is deemed to be lacking capacity, then a 'best interest meeting' takes place (this acts on behalf of the client), and finally the least restrictive option must be put in place in respect of the client's basic rights and freedom. A client's understanding, retention, evaluation and communication of information with regards to the decision must be ensured before a judgement on capacity can be made.

For suggested alternatives, see appendix, page 146.

Structuring paragraphs

For longer pieces of writing it is important to provide the reader with a logical structure. This means that the writing should be divided into paragraphs. Each paragraph has a beginning, middle and end, and contains information on one topic. Therefore, if you change topic, you should start a new paragraph. From this the reader should have a clear sense of the direction in which the writing is going. Paragraphs give the reader a chance to pause and comprehend what has been said before beginning the next paragraph. They are also the building blocks in persuasive writing, providing a line of argument for the reader to follow. Therefore, it is important to keep paragraphs to a regular length and to try to avoid paragraphs which are overly long, as these can indicate that the writer is 'rambling'.

Key sentences

Usually key sentences occur at the beginning of each paragraph and are there to give the reader a clear indication of the topic of the paragraph. This is a very helpful technique to enable the reader to skim quickly through a large document and extract the key points that have been made before closer reading takes place.

Signposting

As a writer you may feel that the direction and structure of your writing is obvious, but as a reader it is very helpful to be told the structure of what you will read – for example, *this report makes three key recommendations, firstly* . . . This is called 'signposting' language. It allows the writer to indicate to the reader that they will be using a certain structure, for example:

- Firstly, secondly, thirdly . . .
- There are four factors to consider . . .
- At first, next, finally . . .
- Then, next, at last . . .
- The main points are outlined below . . .

Try looking at reports written by experienced colleagues to see how and where they use signposting language.

Conjunctions

Conjunctions are words which link two parts of a sentence together. They are useful because they allow you to develop a point or make comparisons. They also help to make writing flow better and show where points compare or contrast.

Common words in this group are:

therefore	so
because	and
thus	nor
or	yet
but	however
thereby	which/that
as a result	nevertheless
although	despite
while	consequently

Subheadings

Subheadings are often used in long documents such as reports to indicate the separate sections. For example, a report might have subheadings such as *aims, methodology, results, discussion*. It is usually very helpful to have subheadings because it enables the reader to get directly to the information they require and it helps the writer to structure their work.

Procedures for distributing documents

Most social work settings will have procedures for distributing written documents, including the need to ensure that they are checked before entering the public domain. You should ensure that documents are sent to recipients in a safe and secure manner and that distribution lists are appropriate. Some documents will have a limited distribution. It is good to be open with information and not restrict it merely to certain, usually senior, members of staff within an organization. On the other hand, many colleagues will probably be grateful if you resist the temptation to distribute every document to everyone, particularly on email where it is easy to 'reply all' or use global distribution lists. It is annoying to be cluttered with information that is not relevant to you. It is important to follow these procedures so that you are sure your writing has met with the standards of your agency and so that you can learn from any feedback you receive. You may find that your place of work has distribution list guidelines or etiquette which you can adopt.

Activity 2.6

Read the extract from a home visit below. Using some of the skills outlined in this chapter, rearrange and edit it using subheadings.

Home visit
Having been allocated to conduct this private fostering assessment, I went to visit T (carer) on 04/03/20XX (T is privately fostering D)

This visit was to gather information about T regarding her childhood, personal experiences, family relationships, meaningful events and the current update on her children. I conducted very creative and interactive work with T, undertaking a Genogram Assessment. I questioned if she feels she is able to care for another child other than her own, based on all the hardships she has faced she was positive she could. I found that her older children had left as they were fed up with T. T expressed that they were old enough to do more around the house, however they did not do anything or provide any help. T was in a difficult circumstance because of this. T's mother assisted the children in finding a place, which T said felt as if she was betrayed because it was done in a secretive way.

We booked to continue with the assessment on 14/03/20XX.

For suggested changes, see appendix, page 146.

Summary

This chapter has situated writing as a fundamental skill within the social worker's repertoire. There are a number of conclusions which can be made. Writing takes effort, but because of the imperative for social workers to communicate clearly, both within and outside of their profession with other colleagues, it is of vital importance. There are many different approaches to writing, and there is no 'right way', but it is useful to reflect on your approach and see if it can be improved by using some of the points outlined in this chapter. One thing of great importance is to have a clear objective for your writing. There are many similarities between writing university assignments and the writing you do as a professional, so as a new social worker you should have confidence in your writing skills, but you should also expect to have support in this area so that you make a successful transition from academic writing to professional writing. Social workers' writing has to be read by a wide audience, so in order for it to be accessible for all, this chapter has recommended structuring your writing carefully, using clear language.

Key points

- Approaches to writing, and the differences between academic and professional writing.
- The skills involved in gathering information.
- The purposes of professional writing.
- Audience, the principles of writing in plain English, and structuring writing.

Further reading and resources

BBC Bitesize *Linking Words of Contrast*, https://www.bbc.co.uk/learningenglish/english/course/towards-advanced/unit-4/session-1.

Buzan, T. (2010) *The Mind Map Book*, London: BBC Books.

Hoobyar, T. and Dotz, T. (2013) *NLP: The Essential Guide to Neuro Linguistic Programming*, London: Harper Collins/William Morrow Paperbacks.

Hopkins, G. (1998) *Plain English for Social Services*, Lyme Regis: Russell House Publishing.

Jones, R. (2012) *Discourse Analysis: A Resource Book for Students*, Hove: Routledge.

Teesside University, *What Makes a Good Sentence?*, https://libguides.tees.ac.uk/sentence

Your Dictionary.com, *Examples of Topic Sentences*, https://examples.yourdictionary.com/examples-of-topic-sentences.html

3 Professional writing

Chapter overview

By the end of this chapter you should have an understanding of:

- general aspects of a professional writing style;
- professional use of language and vocabulary;
- how to apply a professional style to different writing tasks;
- writing tone and anti-oppressive language.

Introduction

This chapter provides general guidance about being objective, accurate and unemotional in your professional writing. It cannot recommend a definitive professional writing style for all social workers because writing style differs depending on the purpose of your writing. You may be writing instructions, describing a process, writing persuasively or summarizing information. This chapter will offer you guidance, but you can also improve your writing style through activities such as:

- Reading other colleagues' reports and assessments critically and learning from their strengths and weaknesses.
- Noticing the features in other people's writing that you admire and that you want your writing to resemble. Even the most experienced writers will use other people's work to inform them about the structure of their own writing.
- Setting aside time to read professionally and for pleasure – textbooks, professional journals, newspapers and novels. The more you read the better your own writing style will become.

The chapter will give examples of different styles used for a range of purposes.

Social workers must demonstrate sound communication skills (QAA, 2019) and consider the implications of the PCF values and ethics domain in professional writing. Part of that is ensuring that the tone, style and expression used in writing is *anti-oppressive*. The chapter gives examples of language which can be interpreted as oppressive and offers suggestions of how this could be expressed in a less oppressive way. Although the social work profession is sometimes accused of political correctness, language is an important indicator of how an issue is viewed. Pugh says, 'Language forms a bridge between the inner self and the external world' (1996, in Bishop 2008). This means that subtle messages are received through written language which can either empower or oppress the reader. This chapter helps you to develop an awareness of language style and tone so that the language you use does not inadvertently oppress.

'Formal language' refers to the level of formality required in professional writing. If you are representing what a service user has said, it is important to be accurate without it being complicated or grandiose. Formal language usually means that phrasal verbs, such as 'put up with' (meaning to endure) or 'call off' (meaning to cancel), should be avoided. It also means that colloquialisms (i.e. regional, conversational language such as 'kids' to mean children and 'brothers' to mean friends) should also be avoided. Idiomatic language such as 'ants in your pants' to mean fidgeting or 'bat out of hell' to mean very fast should, again, be avoided. The professional vocabulary at the end of this chapter is a glossary of terms which have particular meanings in social work and are used in the inter-agency environments of social workers such as children's services, adult community care, mental health, criminal justice, law and education.

General aspects of style

Style refers to the general impression which a piece of writing conveys to its reader. Some writing is deliberately informal, such as text messages or notes. Other writing emphasizes emotion and subjectivity, such as 'opinion pieces' in newspapers. Writing in novels may use colloquialisms and idiomatic language to draw out the characters and situate them in a particular time and place. Writing as a professional social worker requires attention to style to ensure that through your writing a subtle message is conveyed. This message is that there is professional distance, respect for the person and fairness of treatment. It conveys a sense that the professional acts in the service user's interest, but also within a legal framework. This style is objective, concise and unemotional.

Activity 3.1

Read the following extract from a social worker's report and underline any examples of inappropriate style.

X says that part of the problem is that she did not see the point of taking part in Alcoholics Anonymous; however, she has done lots of other things in the meantime. I think this is really good. She said she's tried to contact the kids' school, but it's been like hitting her head against a brick wall. What else can she do? Luckily, we were able to discuss this and make an action plan.

Some of the problems of style can be analysed as follows:

did not see the point of	. . .	imprecise and subjective
lots of other things	. . .	vague
I think	. . .	too personal and subjective
really good	. . .	vague
kids	. . .	colloquialism (avoid)
like hitting her head against a brick wall	. . .	idiom (avoid)
What else can she do?	. . .	question (avoid)
doesn't	. . .	contraction (avoid)
Luckily	. . .	adverb showing personal attitude (avoid)

An exception might be made when you are quoting the service user – for example, *X said she 'did not see the point' of attending Alcoholics Anonymous* . . .

For suggested changes, see appendix, page 147.

Repetition and redundancy

To make your writing flow and sound professional, try to avoid repetition and redundancy. For example, *Many of the residents have commented that the food in the home is often inedible. These residents have also* . . . In the second sentence here, rather than repeat *the residents*, it would be better to use a pronoun, such as *they*.

Redundancy occurs often in speech and sometimes in writing, either because the first meaning is unclear or just as padding for the sentence. This is unnecessary; try to be clear and precise so that redundancy does not occur. For example, *The school has an issue with disruptive behaviour; there is an attitude of troublemaking among a minority of students which causes problems for the whole school. Disruptive behaviour* and *an attitude of troublemaking* mean the same thing, so there is no need to write them both.

Formal language and professional vocabulary

Social workers apply theoretical underpinning within a legal framework on behalf of a service user. Therefore, the language they use must be precise and formal and their vocabulary professional. This helps to establish a professional relationship between the social worker and the service user. While it is important to avoid jargon, formal language can act as a useful boundary which protects social workers and professional vocabulary minimizes the risk of misunderstanding or misinterpretation.

In professional writing precise meaning matters, so it is important to use the right words. Some words are easily confused.

Example

Look at the list below and make sure you are clear about the meaning and spelling of these words. If there are any that you know you confuse, spend some time learning their meaning and spelling.

Word	Means	Confused with	Means
affect	(verb) to act upon or influence Example: *His behaviour affects everyone*	effect	(noun) the result of an action Example: *The effect of his behaviour was long lasting*
affect		affect	(noun) feeling or emotion Example: *Her flat or blunted affect may be a symptom of her psychiatric condition*
cite	(verb) to name Example: *She cited her musical influences as Michael Jackson and Madonna* In academic writing you *cite* sources to support your argument. (You include *citations* in the main body of your work and *references* listed at the end)	site	(noun) the position of something or to position something Example: *The site of the new day centre is not very convenient for people who do not drive*
its	(pronoun) belonging to it Example: *The day centre advertised its Christmas event to all members*	it's	(contraction) it is Example: *It's on Tuesday 20 December*
practise	(verb) to work at or carry out Example: *She has decided to practise mindfulness meditation every day*	practice	(noun) an action or performance Example: *My practice placement is at a local authority children's centre*
principle	(noun) an origin or a rule Example: *The principle behind a 'personalization' approach is to put the service user at the centre*	principal	(adjective) main Example: *Service user participation was the principal message of the article*

Word	Means	Confused with	**Means**
principle		principal	(noun) head of an educational organization Example: *I spoke with the school's principal yesterday*
stationary	(adjective) not moving Example: *The car was stationary when I arrived*	stationery	(collective noun) pens, paper, etc. Example: *I have ordered more stationery for the office*
there	(preposition) in that place Example: *They have lived there for three years*	their	(pronoun) belonging to them Example: *It is their house*
where	in which place Example: *I found him where he said he would be*	were	Past tense of to be Example: *We were together yesterday morning*
whose	Indicates belonging, always followed by a noun Example: *Whose dog is that?*	who's	(contraction) who is Example: *Who's going to the school tomorrow?*
your	Indicates belonging Example: *It is your dog, so you are responsible for its behaviour*	you're	(contraction) you are Example: *You're not allowed to bring dogs into the day centre*

Activity 3.2

Identify words which have been incorrectly used in the following sentences:

1. The effects of the right to buy policy are still being felt today.
2. If the school applies this principal strictly, children with behavioural problems will be excluded from school much more often.
3. The social worker has been practising their profession for the past 15 years.
4. There is no need to prove you're ID in school.
5. There children have been living in care for three and a half months.

For a suggested answer, see appendix, page 147.

Applying professional style to a range of writing tasks

Instructions

Writing instructions is an activity you may be asked to do in your professional role – for example, you may be required to write instructions for a service user to follow. Instructions must always be clear and must not leave out any important items of information. Think, for example, of a cake recipe where vital ingredients such as eggs are left out, or the oven temperature is wrong. This is likely to ruin the entire recipe and make the cake inedible. Therefore, it is important before you write instructions to gather all of the necessary information. Once you have all of the information you need, you should order it and establish the format in which you will present it. A good way to practise writing instructions is to write the directions to get from one place to another. For example, you may need to tell a service user how to find their way to a new venue such as a day centre.

Activity 3.3

Write the directions to a familiar place and give them to a friend to follow. Get your friend to tell you if the instructions you gave were adequate to complete the journey.

Example

From the bus station turn right, follow the road until you come to a T junction. Turn right up Rosemond Street until you come to a red post box. At the post box turn right and walk down the alleyway and under the railway bridge. The day centre is at the end of the alley on the opposite side of the road.

In this example there is a lot of detail, specific information and description; for example, it specifies the colour of the post box, the name of the road and significant features such as the railway bridge. This level of detail helps the reader to be confident that they are going in the right direction. Be careful about using pronouns in description instead of a noun that has already been mentioned or is known (e.g. post box), because the reader might not always be sure what the pronoun is referring to.

Describing a process

Describing a process is similar to writing instructions. There are a number of situations where a social worker may be required to describe a process to a service user – for example, a social worker in an adoption team may have to write to prospective parents to explain the sequence of events leading to a successful adoption placement.

Once the adoption approval is confirmed you will be notified by Social Services. Your details will be placed on the register of approved prospective parents until a suitable child can be matched to you. Once a child has been matched, you will be contacted again by Social Services so that you can read the details of the child. If you are willing to proceed with the adoption process, arrangements will be made for you to meet the child. If you are not willing to proceed, your details will remain on the register of approved parents until another suitable match occurs. If no suitable match is made within a year, you will be required to go through the approval process again in order to update your circumstances.

You will notice that this example has provided a lot of detail of the steps within the process. This is because these scenarios are often very stressful for those involved; therefore, the more detail you can give the better. There is also repeated use of the conditional construction if . . . then . . . For this conditional construction it is important that you ensure your sentences are balanced with a condition and a consequence – for example, *if you are willing to proceed, arrangements will be made.* Notice that in these constructions a comma is placed between the condition and the consequence so that the sentence flows and is comprehensible. It is helpful when writing about these types of processes to try to put yourself in the place of the service user or carer and consider the types of questions and anxieties they may have so that they can be addressed within your correspondence.

Persuasive writing

Sometimes you will be required to write persuasively, such as to advocate for a more comprehensive care plan or to write a positive report for a court appearance.
    Persuasive writing has four core elements:

- it emphasizes the positive aspects of an argument;
- it acknowledges negative aspects, but minimizes them;
- it puts across points strongly;
- it shows commitment.

The example below is a social worker's recommendations to support a boy who needs to move from a mainstream school to a specialist school.

X's parents require support from professionals through the difficult and lengthy process of finding a new school for him. X would benefit from the opportunity of having a safe, structured environment in which to have some enjoyable experiences while a new school is found. The Y Trust can provide this. Although it appears to be an expensive resource (£2,000 for 10 sessions), it has been very effective at supporting children in similar situations. Therefore, it represents good value for money because it will enable X to move successfully to a new school. X's parents are very loving and caring towards X, but they need tangible support to help him to make this traumatic move.

In this example the social worker starts by emphasizing that the situation the family is in is difficult and will take time. This sets the context for the recommendations, which come afterwards. The next sentence argues that the service users need positive experiences during times of transition. The suggestion is for a specific provider to be used because of their track record with other children in similar situations. Although it is mentioned that it is an expensive resource, the language used here is tentative with the use of the passive *although it appears to be expensive*. This is quickly followed by mention of value for money, which is expressed in assertive present simple tense, *this represents good value for money*. Throughout the paragraph adjectives (words to describe things) and adverbs (words to describe actions) are used to give emphasis: *move successfully, tangible support, loving and caring parents*. The last sentence pushes the point made in the first sentence – that the parents need to be supported in this process. This leaves the reader in no doubt about the recommended course of action and the commitment of the social worker to support the child and his parents at a difficult time.

Summarizing – how to build a picture in limited words

In your professional role you will also be required to write summaries. You may be asked to summarize what a service user has said and to pick out key information, or you may have to summarize an entire case for another professional so that they know the key issues and can work with the service user. The essential elements of summary writing are:

1. Make a list of the main issues.
2. Put them into order either by chronology or priority.
3. Make sure you disentangle the key points from extra information such as explanations, excuses, diversions, examples and gossip.
4. Read through your summary to ensure that all the key points are included and that it makes sense.

Activity 3.4

The following extract is taken from an assessment report, but it is too long. Read it and make notes related to the four points above. Then summarize the extract.

X is 7 years old. He generally seems to enjoy good health. He has grown considerably since first entering school. He appears to be tall for his age and is of slight build. He is physically strong, agile and quick. X scored in the low centiles for fine motor and coordination skills. He does not like heights and seems to need quite strong touch to register sensation.
X has a diagnosis of severe ADHD and ASD. His parents and the professionals who know him have doubts that these are helpful labels or that they paint a full picture of X's needs. A diagnosis of attachment difficulties was

removed from his educational statement by a local paediatrician. This was challenged subsequently and remains under debate. X has taken medication for ADHD since the beginning of the school year which may exacerbate his oppositional behaviour. When he is not at school his mother finds that he is able to be calmer without it.

X seems to have an uneven educational profile; this may to some extent reflect his discomfort at being tested. He is having increasing difficulty in managing his emotions which has impacted on his capacity to engage with the curriculum. X appears to be a bright little boy and he has progressed in some areas. He has a very adult mode of speech and he uses a wide vocabulary. This may be a means to help himself feel more in control and can mislead adults into thinking he is more mature than he is. X has had two formal exclusions from school and he is currently not attending school due to the level of physical and emotional stress it is causing him.

X struggles with regulating his emotions; this causes him significant problems and challenges for those looking after him. He carries a sense of sadness and isolation. He is aware of being different without being able to do anything about it. He can't manage the high level of anxiety he experiences, and he is unable to discharge difficult feelings and relax. He gives the impression of always being vigilant. Unfortunately X's strategies for managing his emotions at school often get him into trouble and when a sanction follows (usually in the form of an exclusion) this tends to raise his anxiety further and perpetuates a negative cycle of behaviour.

For a suggested answer, see appendix, page 147.

Analytical language: words and phrases which indicate analysis

The words and phrases that we use can convey our intention. There are certain words and phrases which indicate critical analysis has taken place. As a social worker you are expected to use your professional judgement to analyse cases and question what you see and hear. You are expected to use professional scepticism so that you do not simply accept things as true, but use your professional knowledge and experience to think critically about each case and make suggestions or judgements based on evidence.

The following expressions reflect analysis:

- One question that needs to be asked, however, is whether . . .
- One of the limitations with this is that it does not explain why . . .
- The key problem with this explanation is that . . .
- The existing accounts fail to resolve the contradiction between X and Y . . .
- However, there is an inconsistency with this because . . .
- It seems that X's explanation of Y's injuries is questionable because . . .
- X's interpretation of recent events overlooks much of the physical evidence . . .
- X's analysis does not take account of . . .

More techniques for analytical writing can be found in Chapter 5.

Writing tone and non-discriminatory language

Tone refers to the attitude which is conveyed through language. It is usually easier to tell in spoken dialogue what a person's attitude is, just by the tone they use. In writing, however, it is more difficult to detect tone. This means that you should take care not to write using emotional or emotive language which can expose your bias or prejudices. This is particularly important for social workers who must relate to service users in a non-discriminatory manner. In writing, emphasis can be conveyed through expression, vocabulary and word order. Expression in writing can be quite subtle, but it is important to try to ensure that what you write is as neutral as possible, so that service users do not feel they are being judged. Try to avoid words or expressions with emotional or extreme overtones – if you feel you should use an exclamation mark, the expression is probably inappropriate. Here are some examples of minor adjustments of language that make a significant difference to how the reader understands them.

1. A full risk assessment of this situation needs to be done urgently to ensure the safety and wellbeing of service users.

   not

   This is really important; someone needs to do something about it now, otherwise there will be an accident or death!
2. The onset of dementia means that sometimes the husband behaves in an agitated and frustrated manner towards his wife.

   not

   Because of dementia, the husband is really aggressive and threatening towards his wife.
3. Support is needed to help maintain a clean and hygienic environment at home for children to thrive in.

   not

   The house is always in a very dirty state; it smells bad and is a totally unsuitable environment for children to live in.

Anti-discriminatory practice is a core social work value and it is underpinned in the PCF values and ethics domain (BASW, 2018). There are some important implications for social workers' professional writing. The language that professionals use forms an important part of their professional identity and as such social workers' writing is an important and lasting element of how social work is seen as a profession. Many people who need to use social services are already disadvantaged in society, due to their age, gender, race, location or finances, and these often intersect with one another so that many service users face multiple discrimination. The social worker's role is to minimize discrimination; an important aspect of this is to ensure that all communication, both written and spoken, is as objective and respectful as possible.

Activity 3.5

Read the following examples identifying the elements of the sentences which may feel oppressive to the reader. Rewrite the sentences using less oppressive language.

1. It is clear that most looked-after children do not have a positive experience of education.
2. Good parenting does not occur for most children.
3. This shows that children are . . .
4. This policy makes survivors of domestic abuse feel isolated.
5. Disabled people are less well qualified in comparison to normal people.
6. X is clingy and dependent when her father is around.

For a suggested answer, see appendix, page 147.

Reflection

How would you feel if you read these statements about yourself?

- X is suffering from . . .
  or
  X has a diagnosis of . . .

- X cannot cook independently . . .
  or
  X needs some support with cooking a meal . . .

- X is a victim of domestic abuse . . .
  or
  X is a survivor of domestic abuse . . .

Activity 3.6

Can you rephrase this short extract so that it is less oppressive?

X is disabled which means she has difficulties with normal living skills. She has a brain tumour which has resulted in her being unable to walk. She is wheelchair bound and she is incontinent.

For a suggested answer, see appendix, page 148.

How do you refer to the people you work with?

The terminology used to refer to the people social workers work with is another area for discussion. There are at least three terms in common usage. Decisions about which term to use is often influenced by the setting in which you work.

Service user is probably the most common term used currently; however, some social workers have difficulty with the term 'user', which can sound like drug user. An increasingly used alternative is 'people who use services'. Another term gaining popularity is 'people with lived experience'. Some of these are favoured and used by service user and carer groups.

Although the term **client** is used by some social workers, many feel that it gives the impression of a paying customer who has a choice in the client/professional contract, whereas this is not really the relationship that exists between social workers and service users.

The term **patient** is often used when referring to service users with a mental health condition or a disability, or perhaps with older service users. This is widely rejected by social workers as it seems to represent a medical model that assumes a person has or is a problem due to an illness or condition. Social workers prefer a social model that suggests people are restricted due to the way society is organized, rather than by a person's impairment or difference.

Some professional vocabulary

Precise writing is improved by specific use of vocabulary. If you encounter a new word in a professional setting it is useful to keep a vocabulary log book so that you can build your repertoire of professional vocabulary.

Word	Meaning	Word	Meaning
abnormality	A feature which deviates from typical expectations	intrusive	Imposing on another's time/space
abode	The place where you live	migrant	A person who attempts to relocate permanently to a new country
abuse	To treat someone improperly (e.g. sexually, physically, emotionally, verbally, financially)	miscellaneous	A variety of unrelated things
acute	Sudden and extreme	mobility	The ability to move
adolescence	Transition from childhood to adulthood	modern slavery	Someone who is under the power of another who exercises the rights of ownership over them
advocate	To speak or act on behalf of someone	noncompliance	Refusal to obey

⟶

(continued)

Word	Meaning	Word	Meaning
agoraphobia	Fear of environments (e.g. open spaces) perceived as dangerous or uncomfortable	obsession	Idea which dominates thinking
anxiety	Inner turmoil or stress that can be accompanied by nervous behaviour	onset	Beginning or start/attack
asylum seeker	A person who has been forced to leave their own country because they are in danger and who arrives in another country asking to be allowed to stay there	ostracise	To exclude from a group
behaviour	The way a person acts	panic attack	Sudden rush of fear and anxiety
breakdown	Sudden loss or ability to function (e.g. mental or physical health collapse)	phobia	Irrational and intense fear
chronic	Going on for a long time	preoccupation	Constantly thinking about something
cognitive	Referring to mental or intellectual processes	proactive	Prepare in advance to anticipate a situation
compulsion	An addiction or very strong urge	prostitute	A person who engages in sexual activity for payment
crisis	Time of great danger or difficulty	rapport	Understanding relationship/ communication
custodial	Pertaining to custody (such as prison)	reciprocate	Mutual – to do the same in return
delinquent	Committing an offence (often used for young people)	refugee	A person who has been forced to leave their country in order to escape war, persecution, or natural disaster
depression	Condition of withdrawal or hopelessness	rehabilitate	Restored to action
deteriorate	To get worse	self-esteem	Respect for one's self
disruptive	Bring disorder	sex worker	A person who is employed in the sex industry
empathy	Ability to perceive someone's situation as if you are that person	suicidal	Thinking of killing yourself
gang	Group of people with shared interests, often illegal	survivor	A person who copes with difficulties in their life

(continued)

Word	Meaning	Word	Meaning
harsh	Severe or cruel	tantrum	Fit of childish rage
hostile	Unfriendly or opposed	therapeutic	Beneficial treatment
hyperactive	Abnormally active	trauma	Physical injury or mental shock that has lasting impact
impaired	Inability to undertake certain actions	unaccompanied minor	Child who has been separated from parents and other relatives and is not being cared for by a responsible adult
impulsive	Spontaneous urge to act	victim	A person who has come to feel helpless and passive in the face of misfortune or ill-treatment
inattentive	Lack of attention	vulnerable	At risk
interactions	Communication and personal transactions between people	withdrawn	Quiet or shy
intervention	An action on behalf of someone to effect change		

Summary

This chapter has focused on professional writing style. Although there is not one fixed professional style, it has provided some guidelines to make your writing more professional and to help you to convey a professional identity. Some of the common writing tasks which social workers engage in have been used as examples to demonstrate how to make your writing more formal and concise. The chapter has focused on the style and tone used in formal writing and how, in becoming more aware of this, we are able to make adjustments which establish a professional writing style and ensure that what we write about service users is not oppressive. The chapter should have made you feel more confident about your writing style and more articulate as a professional.

Key points

- Professional style is achieved through precise vocabulary, formal language and unemotive expression.
- Professional tone is an important device for conveying attitude and ensuring anti-oppressive practice.
- You can develop your own professional writing style through reading and reflecting on other colleagues' writing.
- Your writing style will develop and improve with conscious practice.
- You may need to develop more confidence in using formal language and expression.

Further reading

Manchester Academic Phrase Bank, http://www.phrasebank.manchester.ac.uk/being-critical

Professional Word Web, http://www4.caes.hku.hk/vocabulary/tutorial/glossary.asp?sub_subject=Social_Work&sub_subject_ID=7

Wilkins, D. and Boahen, G. (2013) *Critical Analysis Skills for Social Workers*, Maidenhead: Open University Press.

4 Technical aspects of writing

Chapter overview

By the end of this chapter you should have an understanding of:

- some important points of English grammar;
- some important punctuation rules;
- techniques for writing robustly.

Introduction

Writing is an important part of being a professional, so it needs to be easily understood by others and it needs to communicate different things, such as cause and effect, a chronology of events or professional judgements. Mistakes in the use of grammar or punctuation can change the meaning of a sentence and therefore have the potential to lead to misunderstanding and confusion. Therefore, it is important that all of your professional writing is clear and comprehensible.

This chapter covers some of the technical aspects of writing, which include grammar and punctuation. It also has information on how to make your writing more robust by adding qualifying statements and introducing examples. After each explanation there are a few exercises for you to practise your understanding; however, if you feel that you need more practice, you may find specific grammar books useful. There is a list of recommended books and websites at the end of the chapter.

Verb tenses

Verb tenses are the forms of verbs which indicate the time when the action takes place. In order to use verb tenses correctly, you need to be aware of the time you are describing in your writing. Sometimes this is easy, for example:

Yesterday I ate a cheese sandwich for lunch (use the **past simple** for actions in the past which are finished or completed)

In other sentences it is less easy to identify the time reference, for example:

Figure 4.1 The past simple, present perfect and future tenses

The women I met yesterday were talking when I entered the room. They have given me some extra information about my work, which I think you will find very interesting.

The first sentence is in the **past simple**, *met*, because the meeting which took place yesterday is finished. However, the next sentence is in the **present perfect** tense, *have given*, because the action of giving information was in the past but has relevance to the present. The sentence ends with use of the **future** *will*, because the information the women gave is of interest to the listener who has not had that information yet (see Figure 4.1).

The following table shows all of the tenses used in English, gives examples and explains their usage.

Tense	Example	Usage
Present simple	I **walk** to work	For habits For things which are always true For statements
Present continuous	I **am walking** to work	For things which are happening now
Present perfect	I **have walked** to work every day for the past three months	For things which begin in the past but either have relevance now or are continuing to the present
Present perfect continuous	I **have been walking** to work to get fit	For continuing actions which began in the past and continue into the present
Past simple	I **walked** to work yesterday	For past completed actions
Past continuous	I **was walking** to work when I noticed the girl	For describing events in the past which were interrupted by another past event. This tense is often used when telling a story
Past perfect simple	I **had walked** to work every day until I sprained my ankle	To describe two past events, one which preceded the other
Past perfect continuous	I **had been walking** every day before I sprained my ankle	For something which continued for a period of time in the past before another particular point in the past
Future will	I **will** walk to work again when my ankle recovers	To say what will happen in the future (often at an unspecific time)
Future going to	I **am going to** walk to work again next month	To say what is going to happen in the future (often at a particular time)

Activity 4.1

Decide whether the underlined tenses are correct or not.

1. Recently, new evidence relating to this case <u>has emerged</u>.
2. Yesterday the impact of the care order <u>has become</u> obvious.
3. Since the Munro Report, various other cases <u>reached</u> the media.
4. In the last few years, people <u>started</u> to question this approach.
5. Last year no one <u>had realized</u> the importance of this development.

For suggested answers, see appendix, page 148.

Using more than one verb tense within a sentence/paragraph

It is often necessary to use more than one verb tense in a sentence or paragraph. This can sometimes cause confusion. Look at the sentence below and identify the tenses used.

> *Last week service users, who **had** not previously **met**, **attended** an event together. However, as they **began discussing** their experiences, the fire alarm **sounded** so everyone left.*

This can be broken down as follows:

Example	Tense	Why?
had not previously **met**	Past perfect	Fact in the past, before another event in the past
attended	Past simple	Past event which is complete
began discussing	Past perfect continuous	This activity began in the past before the next event in the past
Sounded	Past simple	This event in the past is completed and it also interrupted another event in the past

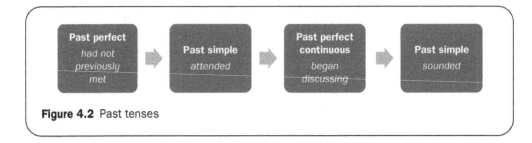

Figure 4.2 Past tenses

Look at the following examples:

1. **Incorrect mixing of past and present tense**

   *The service users **went** into separate rooms so that they **cannot hear** each other.*
   Incorrect. The first verb is in the past tense so the second verb also needs to be in the past tense.

   *The service users **went** into separate rooms so that they **could not hear** each other.*
   Correct. If, however you want to say how something works in general, use the present simple tense:

   *Service users **go** into separate rooms so they **cannot hear** each other.* **Correct.**

2. **Describing one past action followed by another past action**

   *Once we **greeted** the service users we **invited** them to eat.* **Incorrect.**
   *Once we **had greeted** the service users, we **invited** them to eat.* **Correct.**

3. **Misusing the past perfect tense**

   If one action in the past follows another in the past, you need to use the past perfect followed by the past simple to indicate the sequence of events:

   *The boy **had threatened** the teacher before, but last week he **brandished** a knife at her, so he **is** now permanently excluded from school.* **Correct.**

   I arrived at the cinema late last night, the film started already.
   This is **incorrect** because the film had started before you got there. This means that the past perfect should be used to indicate that the film **had started** before you arrived.

4. **Describing something that is generally true**

   Service users with mild depression who follow CBT (Cognitive Behaviour Therapy) strategies recover well. **Correct.**

Activity 4.2

Some of the underlined verb tenses are incorrect. Decide which they are and correct them.

1. It was clear that the family <u>could not continue</u> to function like this.
2. Once the police <u>analysed</u> all of the evidence, they decided not to take matters any further.
3. The AA group was a new experience for her because <u>she had not belonged</u> to a support group before.
4. He talked about experiences in his childhood that <u>have impact</u> on his life now.
5. After the family <u>came</u> to terms with the truth, they were able to rebuild their lives slowly.

For suggested answers, see appendix, page 148.

Subject–verb agreement

In English sentences the subject of the sentence, which is usually a noun or pronoun, has to agree with the verb by either being singular or plural.

He/she/it/the university   starts at 9:00 am
I/they/we/universities   start at 9:00 am

Most of the time we do not have to think about subject–verb agreement because it seems obvious. For example, look at these obvious mistakes:

*The school **allow** (**allows**) pupils to wear non-school uniform on the last day of term.*
*She **recommend** (**recommends**) that we learn as much about the child's background as possible.*

However, there are occasions when the subject–verb agreement is not so obvious. In both of the following sentences there is more than one item in the list. Therefore, the verb 'to be' must be plural – 'are'.

*A calm atmosphere and regular routine **is** recommended for children diagnosed with ADHD.* **Incorrect: replace 'is' with 'are'.**
*Counselling, confidence building, rest and assertiveness training **is** recommended to people who have been in abusive relationships.* **Incorrect: replace 'is' with 'are'.**

Collective nouns such as a class of children, a family or a couple can be confusing, although as these are groups which contain more than one person they are treated as singular in grammar because the collection is singular:

*The child's family **are** very supportive.* **Incorrect.**
*After a lot of consideration, the couple **have** decided to separate.* **Incorrect.**

Activity 4.3

Select the correct verb form for the following sentences.

1. Self-esteem and confidence <u>are/is</u> important for children's development.
2. My collection of papers <u>is/are</u> hidden under the bed.
3. The couple <u>are/is</u> receiving relationship counselling in an effort to save their relationship.
4. Alcoholism and poverty <u>has/have</u> contributed to his breakdown.
5. A small group of young people <u>was/were</u> seen at the scene of the crime.

For suggested answers, see appendix, page 148.

Using noun phrases

Notice the differences in the way these two sentences are expressed:

If the family **can communicate** *better with each other, they* **may prevent** *it from* **being split up** *in a way which* **they find** *undesirable.*
Effective communication *between family members could result in* **the prevention** *of an* **undesirable split**.

The main difference in the grammar of these sentences is that the first is constructed around verbs, whereas the second is based on noun phrases. The effect is that the first sentence sounds partial and subjective, but the second sounds more impartial and objective. This is often useful in professional writing for social workers as they must try to present the facts in an impartial way.

Here are some ways to create noun-based sentences.

1. **Using the noun form of verbs or adjectives**
   The government has criticized the way in which newspapers **have covered** *high profile domestic violence cases.*
   The government has criticized the newspapers' **coverage** *of high profile domestic violence cases.*

   The police often question **how reliable** *young witnesses can be.*
   The police often question the **reliability** *of young witnesses.*

2. **Using a noun with the same meaning as a phrase**
   It is often possible to replace a phrase with a single word instead. This usually has the effect of making the writing sound more precise and formal, for example:

   A couple of members of the jury doubted whether the father's improved behaviour **could be kept going.**
   A couple of members of the jury doubted **the sustainability** *of the father's improved behaviour.*

3. **Using the 'ing' form of a verb**
   It is possible to use an ing ending to make a sentence sound more direct and avoid conditional sentences which can sound judgemental, for example:

   If the house **were cleaned,** *it would be a better environment for children to live in.*
   Cleaning *the house would make it a better environment for children to live in.*

Activity 4.4

Complete these sentences with noun phrases:

1. The school has decided to <u>construct</u> a new centre dedicated to pupils with behavioural problems.

The .... of a new centre will be dedicated to pupils with behavioural problems.

2. The judge questioned whether some of the evidence given by police was <u>relevant</u>.
   The judge questioned the .... of some of the evidence given by police.

3. Community groups were <u>satisfied</u> when they heard the announcement.
   Community groups greeted the announcement with ....

4. The council's provision of social housing <u>has been getting better</u> in recent years.
   There has been an .... in the council's provision of social housing in recent years.

For suggested answers, see appendix, page 149.

Commas

Commas can be tricky to use, but they are often important for the sense of the writing. There are five main rules which govern the use of commas. Some of these rules are well known, others are less well understood.

1. **To separate items in a list.**
   A comma is placed after each item on a list:
   The social worker talked to the service user about housing, health and education issues.

   If items within a list require more than one word they are more likely to be separated with a semicolon:
   The social worker talked to the service user about the housing issues she faces; her ongoing health concerns and her education options.

2. **In sentences with conjunctions (linking words)**
   A comma should be used before these conjunctions: for, and, nor, but, or, yet, so – to separate two independent clauses (this group of conjunctions is often remembered by the mnemonic FANBOYS). They are called 'coordinating conjunctions':
   The social worker had talked to her about housing, but the issue of her ongoing health concerns had not been discussed.
   The girl said she felt lonely and depressed, so she used alcohol to lessen those feelings.

   Do not use a comma if the information following the conjunction is not an independent clause:
   My sister and I went to the fair on Saturday. I went on all the rides but she didn't.

Exception: if you use 'however' in the middle of two independent clauses it should be enclosed by commas:
I like going on rides at the fair, however, my sister is terrified of them.

3. **To separate introductory elements of a sentence**

Introductory elements can be short, using just one word such as however, therefore, nevertheless, or they can be longer using an introductory phrase:
However, it is important to resolve the housing issues before anything else can be addressed.
Although they had spent a long time discussing housing issues, they were not able to resolve the matter to a satisfactory conclusion.

4. **To give additional information within a sentence**

This is useful if you want to add describing or additional information within a sentence. This is often the type of information that could go into brackets, but a pair of commas is often more readable:
The relationship between the husband and wife, which had been antagonistic and destructive, has now deteriorated into violence.

5. **Commas are also used before writing direct speech**

For example:
Mary said, 'I love going to the cinema.'

Activity 4.5

Insert the commas into this paragraph.

On 17 January 20XX having failed to report to the police station X was caught on CCTV camera shoplifting food. In a statement given later that day X said 'I was hungry and I didn't have any money so I had to get something to eat.' Although this is a breach of X's bail order it is the first time that something like this has happened and he has shown immediate remorse. There is also evidence of significant improvement in his behaviour at school home and with friends.

For a suggested answer, see appendix, page 149.

Semicolons and colons

There are two uses for the semicolon: these are to separate complicated items in a list and to join two independent clauses (sentences).

1. **To separate complicated items in a list**

   Most lists only require commas to separate items within them, however some are more complicated. In these cases it is perfectly acceptable to use semicolons to make the items clear. Some items in a list themselves require commas. This can make for difficult reading – for example, look at the following sentence:
   Those present at the professionals' review meeting were PC Harris, Metropolitan Police, Dr Potter, NHS trust, Ms Jones, Senior Social Worker and Mrs Abdul, the boy's mother.

   This can be made easier to read by using semicolons to separate each individual:
   Those present at the professionals' review meeting were PC Harris, Metropolitan Police; Dr Potter, NHS trust; Ms Jones, Senior Social Worker and Mrs Abdul, the boy's mother.

2. **To separate closely related independent clauses**

   Some independent clauses – i.e. complete sentences – are closely related in content. This can be indicated by the use of a semicolon instead of a full stop. For example:
   She was attacked on her way home from a school netball match; she is now terrified of going out at night.
   Everything seems easier when you are on holiday; there's less stress and you can put life into perspective.

3. **Colons are used to introduce a list**

   The main factors which influence happiness are: stress, money, relationships and work.

Activity 4.6

Punctate the following sentences.

1. There are some wonderful towns to visit in Kent such as Canterbury with its ancient Cathedral Whitstable famous for oysters and Dover known throughout the world for its white cliffs.
2. The attendees at today's meeting included Mr Bentley PCS Mrs Fry head teacher and Janet Patel senior social worker.
3. All the way home he complained of a headache he had been hit on the head by a football during the match at school.
4. It's easier to support a family who have volunteered for the programme they have often discussed many of the issues which can cause conflict.
5. Nobody at the child's school had seen him for over a week this is often the case in these situations.

For a suggested answers, see appendix, page 149.

Apostrophes

Apostrophes are a small but important punctuation mark. They either indicate that some letters are missing from words or that there is possession. Misuse of apostrophes can sometimes change the sense of a sentence and lead to confusion. For example:

> *The girls bags were on the back of the bus when a bomb went off* – is this the bags of one girl or more than one girl?
> *The mothers cries could be heard across the playground* – is this one mother or many?
> *The cars wheels really needed to be changed* – is this one car or many cars?

1. **For contractions**

   In speech many words are contracted to speed up pronunciation. In writing it is possible to indicate this contraction by putting an apostrophe in place of the missing letter or letters. However, in formal or professional writing it is better to write out the words in full, so it is unlikely that you will need to use apostrophes to indicate contractions in your writing at work.

   - he is – he's
   - she is – she's
   - is not – isn't
   - was not – wasn't
   - does not – doesn't
   - cannot – can't
   - you are – you're

2. **To indicate possession**

   This is the only other use for apostrophes, but it can cause some confusion, especially when there is an irregular plural like children, women or mice.

   In general, an apostrophe and an 's' is placed after the noun to show that something belongs to that noun:

   The table's legs are intricately patterned.
   The girl's hair was tied in a ponytail.
   The school's policy is no make-up at all.

   These are all singular nouns and the apostrophe shows possession. It is also possible for plural nouns to show possession. This is done by placing the apostrophe after the 's':

   The cars' exteriors had been highly polished.
   The social workers' Christmas party was more fun this year than last year.
   The boys' clothes were scattered all over the house.

   For irregular plurals the apostrophe is placed after the noun and an 's' is added:

   The children's dinner is served at 7:00 pm.
   Women's netball matches take place once a month on the school playground.

Men's health is a concern for GPs.

Note: it is incorrect to put apostrophes in dates (such as 1980s) or to show plural for abbreviations (such as GPs).

Activity 4.7

Insert apostrophes in the correct places in the following sentences.

1. The impact of lack of exercise on childrens weight is evident in growing levels of obesity.
2. Apples latest iPhone has become the most commonly stolen item in schools.
3. Teenagers behaviour is influenced by their peers.
4. Ive always preferred cheese and onion crisps to other flavours.
5. The role of art is to challenge peoples ideas rather than to paint pretty pictures.

For suggested answers, see appendix, page 149.

Activity 4.8

Correct the following sentences by inserting or removing apostrophes where necessary.

1. The CQCs inspection took place last week so the office was in disarray.
2. Baby Ps case marked a watershed in social work practice.
3. Munros' recommendations have had far-reaching implications.
4. The social work profession has changed beyond recognition from what it was in the 1970's.
5. Elderly people in their 80's and 90's are now expected to manage their own care.

For suggested answers, see appendix, page 150.

Robust writing techniques

As a social worker you will be required to make arguments and advocate on a service user's behalf. If this is in writing, it requires robust writing techniques such as adding qualifying statements and introducing examples.

Adding qualifying statements

It is important not to overstate your case because readers will easily detect when you are making false or exaggerated claims. It is better to use hedging language (see Chapter 2) when introducing a qualifying statement, so that the reader knows that there are limits to your claims.

There are various ways that you can qualify a statement.

1. **Use phrases which show there are/were reasons why something has happened**
   To some extent *a healthy diet and regular bedtime has had a positive impact on X's behaviour.*

2. **Use phrases which show how something is true**

   *A healthy diet and regular bedtimes have led to better behaviour **in the sense that** X no longer attacks other children or has tantrums.*

3. **Use phrases that clarify which aspect of the statement is true**

   In terms of *X's behaviour, a healthy diet and regular bedtimes seem to have had more impact than firm rules and sanctions.*

Other phrases that can help to qualify a statement include:

- To some extent
- To some degree
- In the sense that
- To the extent that
- In terms of
- In that
- Insofar as

Activity 4.9

Qualify each statement in a single sentence using the words in the brackets.

1. (in the sense that) Sex education has been successful. Rates of teenage pregnancy in the UK have fallen.
2. (in that) Sure Start failed. The people accessing it were not the most in need.
3. (to the extent that) The Munro report was useful. It highlighted shortcomings in inter-agency working.
4. (insofar as) The outcome for these children is positive. They have been placed in long-term foster care.
5. (in that) Provision of physiotherapy for elderly people is cost-effective. It can extend their ability to live independently.

For suggested answers, see appendix, page 150.

Introducing examples

In order to strengthen your writing and add weight to an argument it helps to give an example. There are a number of ways in which this can be done.

1. **Use the word 'example'**

   Many schools in this town are working in partnership with social services. A good example of this is the new academy which employs a social worker on a .5 contract to work with looked-after children at the school.

2. **Use phrases: 'for example', 'for instance'**

   Many schools in this town, for example the new academy, now employ social workers.

3. **Use 'such as', especially for lists**

   Many schools in this town such as: W academy, X academy, The Y school and Z girls' school employ a social worker to support at-risk children.

4. **Use phrases connected with the word 'illustrate'**

   In this town, partnerships between schools and social services have become much more common. This is illustrated by the growth of posts for social workers now advertised within schools.

Activity 4.10

The following paragraph is taken from a newly qualified social worker's self-appraisal. Rewrite it using a range of techniques to introduce examples.

Some aspects of my first year as a social worker working in the leaving care team have been positive. Initially I was given a caseload of eight children. This gave me a chance to find information about those children. I got to know their interests and understand their situations as well as talking with them about their career or education plans. I enjoyed this experience and I felt I was doing a good job. I received positive feedback from my supervisor. Since Christmas my caseload has doubled and I have not had time for weekly supervision. This has caused me some stress and anxiety. I do not feel that I know the children as well and I am unable to give them the person-centred service that they require.

For a suggested answer, see appendix, page 150.

Summary

This overview of some of the technical aspects of grammar and punctuation hopefully will have reminded you of some rules in English language. These are useful in ensuring your writing is comprehensible and your audience is not distracted by mistakes. Although some punctuation is a matter of opinion, it is helpful to know the basic rules and avoid the most common errors. It is also essential that you develop a habit of reviewing your written work and reading your writing before it is shared with others.

Often you can detect mistakes by reading work aloud (although if you do this in an open-plan office, it may perhaps be unpopular with your colleagues). You should always try to proofread your work and be vigilant for spelling, grammar and punctuation errors. In addition to these mistakes your writing will also benefit if you ask yourself the question: 'Have I said this as clearly and precisely as possible?' Finally, try to learn from others' writing by paying attention to how their use of grammar and punctuation helps or hinders you as a reader.

The section on robust writing techniques introduced you to the idea that there are ways in which you can strengthen your writing to make it more convincing to the reader. Given that a social worker's role often involves advocacy on behalf of a service user, these techniques are invaluable tools for professional life.

Key points

- Some basic errors in punctuation can lead to confusion.
- Understanding the rules of grammar helps you to write in a more professional style.
- Techniques that make your writing more robust are essential for successful professional life.

Further reading

Bristol Online Grammar, Faculty of Arts, www.bristol.ac.uk/arts/exercises/grammar/grammar_tutorial/page_41.htm

English Grammar Online, www.ego4u.com/en/cram-up/grammar/phrasal-verbs

Harrison, M., Jakeman, V. and Paterson, K. (2012) *Improve Your Grammar*, Basingstoke: Palgrave Study Skills.

Lynch, J. (n.d.) *Guide to Grammar and Style*, Rutgers University, https://andromeda.rutgers.edu/~jlynch/Writing.

Oxford dictionary, www.askoxford.com

Sinclair, C. (2010) *Grammar: A Friendly Approach*, Maidenhead: Open University Press.

Trask, L. (n.d.) *Guide to Punctuation*, University of Sussex, www.sussex.ac.uk/informatics/punctuation

Part 2

Applying professional writing to social work practice

5 Critical analysis in professional writing

Chapter overview

By the end of this chapter you should have an understanding of:

- how to use the information you gather from practical social work situations to construct an analytical piece of writing to support service users;
- the difference between making a judgement and being judgemental in your writing;
- what critical writing is and how it is linked to critical thinking.

Introduction

Thus far this book has focused on the technical aspects of good writing and has provided context-based practice of some of the more difficult areas of English usage. Through this practice you should feel more confident about the rules of English language and the conventions of professional writing. This part of the book focuses on the application of these skills in particular writing tasks common to social work, such as correspondence, records, reports and funding applications. This chapter on critical writing underpins all of these topics and is the key to professional thinking and writing in social work. PCF6 (BASW, 2018) highlights applying 'critical refection and analysis to inform and provide a rationale for professional decision-making' as a core social work skill.

Critical analysis is now the generally accepted basis for good decision-making, however there has been debate over the years about the advantages of analytical versus intuitive decision-making. This debate has been particularly contested in caring professions such as nursing and social work. Intuitive practice is based on personal and experiential responses to individuals and issues, whereas analytical practice is based on a step-by-step logical and defensible process (Hammond, 1996). Although it is now widely accepted that intuitive practice is hazardous because it is inherently flawed by bias, it would not be right to remove intuition completely from social workers' decision-making processes. Hammond suggests that intuition and analysis should be used together to help make sound decisions. For example, a social worker may be faced with a service user who is experiencing high levels of domestic violence at home, and is using alcohol to cope with this situation. The social worker's intuition may tell her that the service user is unlikely to break that cycle of behaviour if their alcohol dependency is not addressed first, however in order for this to be recommended the social worker will need to analyse all the factors present in the service user's life so that a rational recommendation is agreed.

Some social work involvement will be straightforward and the action that you and other professionals take on behalf of the service user will be obvious, but in many cases – involving mental health issues, care proceedings and risk assessments – there might be conflicting evidence, or issues may change and develop over time and therefore the best course of action is not obvious. Within the profession now there is an emphasis on what Saleeby (2012) calls strength-based practice so social workers need to work with service users to identify their strengths and put interventions in place on these strengths. As the social worker you will need to use your professional judgement to weigh up the facts and come to a reasoned conclusion. Often the process of writing this down can help you to think through the evidence and structure an argument so that your response is justified to the service user and other professionals involved in the work. Swales and Feak (2012) refer to this style of writing as an *analytical and rhetorical* approach. This means that analytical skills are applied to persuasive communication within a professional discourse such as social work.

Making judgements or being judgemental

There can be confusion for students and new social workers about the difference between making a judgement and being judgemental. Making a judgement involves an informed decision based on evidence, facts or observation. For example, if a service user is misusing drugs you would discuss the risks associated with this, but you would not label that service user as 'wrong' or 'injudicious' because this is judgemental. A judgemental attitude causes a person to reach a conclusion based on personal bias or misplaced moral authority rather than based on evidence. Recent work by Firmin (2020) on child protection has highlighted the need for social workers to take account of the environmental context in which the abuse of young people occurs. She encourages social workers to focus on the places, times and spaces where abuse occurs rather than only problematizing the victim and the abuser. Therefore, it is important to remember that a judgemental attitude can say more about you than it does about the person you are judging.

Much of what social workers write is used as the basis for making complex and often difficult decisions about people's lives. Therefore, just reporting the facts relating to a piece of work is not enough to guide a good decision. Social workers are expected to use their professional knowledge and experience to critically analyse facts. This means that you must process the evidence that you gather and arrange it into a sequence that can help to make informed decisions. Critical writing acts as a written argument where the conclusions which are drawn are reached on the basis of the logically presented evidence.

The case for the importance of critical analysis was made very strongly in a family law case by Dyson et al. (2014) in the Court of Appeal. The judges in this case found that they were unable to make a ruling because of the lack of analysis provided by the social worker. They were very concerned by what they described as 'sloppy practice' in an adoption case and went on to say that they had, 'searched without success in the papers for any written analysis'. They recommended two essential elements in considering adoption cases: firstly, 'proper evidence' and secondly, 'adequately reasoned judgements'. Although the comments relate to adoption proceedings, they underline the vital role all social workers play in gathering evidence and then setting it out before the courts or other decision-making bodies so that both sides of an argument can been seen and a reasoned judgement can be made.

In current social work practice, reports and assessments are increasingly prepared on computer templates and many social workers report that they feel constrained by these. Templates may make documents easier to read because information is always in the same place; however, they can have a tendency to result in information which is standardized and bland and may not be that useful for critical analysis. Therefore, when you are presented with an opportunity to write 'free text' you should use it to convey information on your assessment of a situation, include critical analysis of the evidence and a rationale for the decisions you have made.

What is critical writing?

Critical writing goes beyond description to evaluate evidence in order to reach a conclusion or recommendation. It should give a balanced argument presenting why the conclusion has been reached and acknowledging any limitations within it. It should set out a rationale for the argument which is being made. Critical writing uses similar skills to those used in reflection, which are:

* identifying significant issues;
* weighing up positives and negatives;
* considering the role of emotions;
* finding out other perspectives;
* thinking hypothetically about other actions;
* challenging assumptions;
* applying this thinking throughout your professional interactions.

The table below shows the differences between descriptive and analytical writing. It is adapted from Cottrell (2003: 232), and shows how you can develop your writing from basic factual description to a deeper consideration and structured evaluation of the evidence, which will be much more helpful to other professionals who may have to understand your reasoning based simply on what you have written.

Descriptive writing	Critical analytical writing
States what happened	Identifies the significance of what happened
Gives the story so far	Weighs one piece of information against another
Says how to do something	Argues a case according to evidence
Explains what a theory says	Shows why a theory is relevant or suitable in this situation
Explains how something works	Indicates why something will work, or work best
Says when something occurred	Identifies why the timing is of importance
States options	Gives reasons for selecting each option
Lists issues in a random order	Structures information in order of importance
States links between items	Show the relevance between pieces of information
Gives information	Draws conclusions

In order to help you to structure your own critical thinking and writing, this chapter focuses on six steps in critical writing:

1. Gather as much evidence as you can.
2. Check for bias and assumptions: view the issues from other perspectives.
3. Select and justify the inclusion of information so that your intervention can be looked at holistically.
4. Identify your main line of reasoning and ensure that you support recommendations with strong evidence. This is often referred to as developing a 'professional voice'.
5. Explore weakness: think about counter-arguments which other professionals may raise, and prepare to defend your decisions.
6. Limit the conclusion: do not make recommendations that are inflexible unless they can be defended.

Gather as much evidence as you can

Finding the right evidence relating to an individual or a family with whom you are working is fundamental to resolving an issue fairly. In a 1999 paper titled 'Common errors of reasoning in child protection work', Munro found that social workers often based their assessments on a narrow range of evidence and were frequently persuaded by first impressions or the most memorable events rather than by what she called 'consistent and careful fact gathering'. However, it is not enough just to present all of the evidence available. Your role is also to *interpret* for the reader what is going on. This interpretation will be based on analysis of the evidence, but also on your professional knowledge, skills, ethics and experience. Your interpretation of the evidence will not necessarily be exactly the same as another social worker's interpretation, and it is unlikely to be the same as another professional such as a solicitor, teacher, health professional, police or probation officer. This lack of consistency does not invalidate the decisions indi-vidual social workers make but it does reinforce the need for you to be able to defend your decisions by tracking back and explaining why you acted in the way that you have. It is also important at an early stage in critical writing to check for your own personal bias and assumptions (this links to point 2 below).

Finding more detail

After you have done an initial assessment with a service user and their family (if appropriate), it is very important to review the notes that you have made and reflect on them. You should look at the information you have gathered and then try to fit that into your pre-existing knowledge on a topic. For example, you may have visited a woman who has disclosed that she is living with a violent partner. It will be important for you to gather your knowledge of domestic violence, for example:

- think about the options that this woman has available to her;
- consider the impact domestic violence will have on the woman and on other members of her family;
- consider the impact it may have on the woman's ability to work and to interact with friends;
- assess the woman's ability to effectively access primary services such as health and education.

It is important that you tap into your internal monologue to see how you are pro-cessing information after an initial assessment or meeting. Therefore, it is also useful to carry a small notebook at all times so that you can jot down ideas and thoughts as they arise.

While you are assessing service users it is important that you are aware of the potential for your own assumptions to filter information. A weakness that Munro (1999) identified in her report on social workers' errors in reasoning was that although social workers are able to be sceptical about new evidence which con-flicts with their existing view of a situation, they can be too accepting of evidence if it supports their existing view. This means that they are likely to be unwilling to change their mind about a service user or a situation even when new evidence suggests that they should.

Example

A child's mother has been in hospital for two weeks with a diagnosis of depres-sion. She is out of hospital now but still very fragile; she remains on medication which makes her drowsy and she has a lot of practical issues to arrange due to the break-up of her relationship which is emotionally draining and for which she is receiving therapeutic support. Therefore, she will find it difficult to cope with the demands of caring for a 3-year-old child.

In this case, it is recommended that the child goes into respite care for two weeks to allow her mother time to recover from her own illness; however, the woman may recover quicker than had been assumed and may also find that caring for her child is a useful focus away from her depression. In this case it may be necessary for the social worker to question their own assumptions about the need for respite care and instead put in place support for the mother to care for her child while she recovers. This process will need to be recorded in writing so that other professionals can see how decisions were made and as a record for the social worker and service user.

To find out more detail it is not essential to note verbatim all of the information in each case. Try instead to get an understanding of why things are happening as they are and then apply your professional knowledge to them. This will involve asking the right questions, such as:

- Is there any information missing from my notes?
- Has the service user tried to manipulate my thinking?
- Has the service user made any claims which cannot be justified?
- Why might they have done this?
- What issues are raised within this scenario?
- What do I know and think about these issues?
- Does this case have similarities with other cases I have worked on?
- What did I learn from them?

Activity 5.1

Use the questions above to reconsider a case you have been involved in recently. Do any of the questions make you reconsider your previous assumptions or thoughts about the case?

Social work operates within legal and policy frameworks which protect both the service user and the social worker; therefore, it is of utmost importance that for each person you work with you consider the legal and policy framework. This will help you to take into account other perspectives as well, since you will have to think about the case from a legal or policy perspective. For example, in the case of adoptions, appeals by the birth parent against an adoption are permitted until the adoption has been approved. After this, even if new evidence is found or the birth parent's circumstances change for the better, making them a more suitable parent, the decision cannot be reversed due to the disruptive impact that this may have on the child. This emphasizes the importance of social workers considering all options in a case.

Check for bias and assumptions: view the issues from other perspectives

This chapter has already highlighted the criticism made by Munro (1999) that social workers are often reluctant to revise their initial opinions about a service user. Munro says that judgements based on an assumption or bias are open to weakness. You will need to check what you have written and think about whether there is unconscious bias or assumptions which are not readily apparent or that you have been unaware of. One way of checking for assumptions and bias is to ask another colleague's opinion on what you have written. This may form part of the supervision process. Another strategy to help social workers examine their assumptions is suggested by Munro, who asks them to try and imagine that they are somebody who takes the opposing view of a service user to their own, and to think of reasons why their initial opinion might be wrong. For this approach it is useful to think of questions that challenge your assumptions.

Example

You are a new social worker on a case of a teenage mother who lives in a comfortable home with her own parents and is studying for her A levels.

In this example, you have made the assumption based on your initial home visit to the teenager and her baby that she is well supported and will be able to cope with the demands of parenting and continuing her own education. Therefore, she does not need the involvement of social services. However, the teenager's form teacher has raised serious concerns about this arrangement because of her long-term involvement with and knowledge of the girl and her family. The following questions may help you to question your assumptions here:

• What would you think if you knew the parents were absent from home for long periods while they stayed in their holiday home in Spain?
• What would you think if you knew the teenager's older brother, who still lives at the family home, has a criminal record for sexually abusing a minor?
• What would be your concerns if you knew that the teenager's boyfriend (the baby's father) was a drug dealer at the school?
• How might you react if you saw that the teenager had a history of mental health issues including anorexia, self-harm and depression?
• What would you think if you knew that the girl had successfully concealed the pregnancy until the delivery?

After considering these questions you are unlikely to be as sure of your decision as you were, so you will need to do further assessments with the girl and her family network to fully ensure that she is capable of looking after her baby and that she has appropriate support.

Example

Children are currently residing with their mother, but she is struggling to cope because of her alcohol dependency and precarious financial circumstances. It is therefore recommended that the children be placed in temporary care until she is more stable.

This argument may seem fine on the surface, but there may be an unconscious bias towards putting children into care if no attempt has been made to find out whether the children's father is willing and able to care for the children while their mother recovers.

This section on checking your own assumptions for bias is a very important aspect of professional practice for social workers. Although as Hammond (1996) noted, decisions are made based on a combination of intuition and analysis, you should always check that you are not becoming rigid in your decisions. It is essential for social workers to review the decisions they make and be open to changing their minds. Munro (1999) reminds us that changing your mind should be considered as *good practice* – a strength, not a weakness. Remember, your aim is to identify and exclude your own judgemental responses and instead build an argument which uses evidence in order to make a reasoned and supported judgement.

Select and justify the inclusion of information so that your intervention can be looked at holistically

Your reports will need to cover the main points of a case, so it is essential to identify what is important! If you include too much information, it will be impenetrable for the reader and you risk the audience being unable to see the whole picture and so miss the point of your argument. However, if you leave out vital information there may not be enough evidence upon which to base a decision. Therefore, you must select the information that you include in your critical writing and explain logically why you have presented this information. Munro (1999) recommends that social workers stand back from the case they are working on in order to be able to place current events into a longer-term assessment. Try not to assume that your reader will use the same logic as you or will be able to work out what to do without explanation. For this it may be helpful to view a case in terms of *problem–process–solution* (Swales and Feak, 2012: 100).

For example, the problem is a woman in hospital with multiple fractures as a result of domestic violence. The process of arriving at that problem may have been:

- husband loses his job;
- wife needs to support family so gets a full-time job;
- husband becomes reclusive and depressed;
- husband does not seek medical help for depression and instead starts problem drinking;
- arguments between husband and wife increase;
- family in financial difficulty; repossession order on house and reliance on food bank;
- arguments become violent on both sides;
- wife in hospital with multiple fractures.

The structure in which you present information has an impact on those other professionals using your reports. A step-by-step, *problem–process* account is useful for explaining why something has happened, but it may not be so useful when setting out a range of possible solutions. For this McFarlane (2013, cited by Dyson et al., 2014) recommends that social workers should present solutions in a holistic rather than a linear way:

> The linear approach . . . is not apt where the judicial task is to undertake a global holistic evaluation of each of the options available for the child's future upbringing before deciding which of these options best meets the duty to afford paramount consideration to the child's welfare.

McFarlane warns that if social workers present options as a list of unacceptable choices, the result will be that an unsatisfactory solution will be chosen rather than a solution based upon a holistic consideration of options that may work together.

In the adoption case mentioned earlier in this chapter (Dyson et al., 2014) the social worker did not support the adoption or removal of the child, but neither did she make a strong case against these options. In fact, the Court of Appeal judges' criticism was that there was insufficient rationale for any decision to be made. It was explained that the positives and negatives of the case for and against removal from the parent needed to be set out by the social worker before a fair judgement could be reached:

> I have searched without success in the papers for any written analysis by local authority witnesses or the guardian of the arguments for and against adoption and long term fostering . . . Care should always be taken to address this question specifically in the evidence/reports and that this was not done here will not have assisted the judge in his determination of the issue.
>
> (Dyson et al., 2014)

This is a very robust criticism of the social worker's court report and reveals an underlying frustration that some judges have with the lack of critical analysis which is being undertaken by social workers.

Judges argue that without access to the social worker's analysis it is impossible for them to make a reasoned judgement on something as important as the residency of a child. This means that social workers have considerable influence in court decisions and this should be used to help achieve social justice on behalf of service users. However, as mentioned earlier, it is becoming increasingly common for social work reports to be done using online templates. These are often highly structured documents with small spaces to input information. This can be a constraint to a social worker, so the following tips from experienced professionals on making the most of any 'free text' opportunities may be useful:

- always use the free space;
- do not waffle – get straight to the point;
- use noun-based sentences (e.g. 'The child requires weekly therapy');
- be specific (e.g. 'The therapy must be weekly, for one hour and it must focus on developing coping strategies');
- if the free text space is insufficient, add an appendix to the document;
- identify your main line of reasoning and ensure that you support recommendations with strong evidence – develop a professional voice (see below).

Identify your main line of reasoning and ensure that you support recommendations with strong evidence (often referred to as developing a 'professional voice')

In order to construct a strong argument it is necessary to build up reasons which lead logically to the final conclusion or recommendation. The more reasons which can be given the better and the reasons will need to be strong and logical, not based on assumptions or weak analogies. A logical line of reasoning is sometimes referred to as a 'professional voice' which you will develop as you become a more experienced social worker. Having a professional voice means that you speak and write formally and with authority, and that you have an awareness of the power relations between yourself and your audience.

Writing that conveys a professional voice is evident when the writer's stance can be discerned by the reader. In other words, a piece of writing which expresses a professional voice will be writing that has a clear purpose. This emphasizes the need for professional writing to be planned and to allow time for writing tasks that require your professional voice to be heard – for example, in court reports or care proceedings. In the often pressured environments in which social workers operate, allowing enough time for writing tasks may have to be negotiated with managers so that you do not feel under too much pressure to write quickly. It requires time to write a report or recommendation which will help others to arrive at an informed opinion quickly.

Example

Mrs X is 95. She has been in hospital for two weeks due to difficulties eating, severe indigestion and dietary deficiencies. She remains malnourished and underweight, having lost a further 5 kg while in hospital. She has mobility difficulties and is partially sighted, so she is no longer able to cook a simple meal for herself. Therefore it is recommended that she have a carer visit three times a day to prepare meals for her and help her to eat.

In this example, what arguments are given for recommending care three times a day?

* remains malnourished;
* lost weight in hospital;
* mobility difficulties;
* partially sighted.

Arguments can be strengthened by extending the reasons or evidence that you present to make a conclusion, or by an interim conclusion before a final conclusion or recommendation is made.

Explore weaknesses: think about counter-arguments which other professionals may raise, and prepare to defend your decisions

Sometimes as a social worker you will have to argue against other professionals who have different arguments. It is always useful to imagine a counter-argument so that you can prepare your defence and spot any weaknesses in your own argument. You will also get better at identifying flaws in other people's arguments. Here are some examples of weak arguments. One obvious area of weakness is *confusing causes with consequences*. An example of this is:

> The reason that Mrs X is an unfit mother is because she was brought up in a violent home, therefore she cannot provide a safe environment for her own child.

This is a weak argument; just because a person was exposed to a violent home as a child, this does not mean it will automatically result in a violent home for his or her own children. You will need to be able to spot weak arguments and challenge them. You will also need to ensure that your own arguments are robust and do not jump to conclusions.

Some weak arguments are termed 'slippery slope' arguments because they move very quickly from the current factual position to a hypothetical negative scenario. Here is an example.

Example

If child A is removed from her parent, she is unlikely to be placed in a permanent family setting because she is 9 years old and from a black and minority ethnic (BME) background. Therefore, she will go into care which will be disruptive. It is likely to have a negative impact on her school performance and she may be more likely to miss school due to peer pressure and lack of motivation. This may then result in her dropping out of school or becoming involved in the criminal justice system.

This argument is weak because it moves too quickly from being against removal of a child to that child dropping out of school or getting involved in the criminal justice system. In this situation it is better not to speculate about the possible consequences of a decision.

Example

If child A is removed from her parent, she is unlikely to be placed in a permanent family setting because she is 9 years old and from a BME background. This may have a disruptive impact upon the child.

Another example of a weak argument is known as a 'straw man' argument. This essentially means that the main argument is ignored and instead another tangential argument is built which can easily be blown down (like a straw man). This distracts your audience and allows your argument through.

Example

Children at school are becoming increasingly disruptive. They are unmotivated in class and they seem to expect that the teachers will deliver everything on a plate to them. Most children no longer want to work hard to get good results, instead they think that all of the answers can be found on the internet so they can't be bothered to do any real thinking. Therefore, teachers' unions are appealing for more support from head teachers to control discipline in class.

This argument starts with a comment on children's disruptive behaviour and then distracts us with irrelevant information about children's lack of motivation. The main point of the argument – that teachers' unions need more support from head teachers – is then at odds with what went before it.

A final style of argument which you may encounter, but which is also weak, is the 'appeal to popularity'. This type of argument relies on popular opinions rather than analysis or logic and should be easy to spot.

Example

Most people conform to gender roles quite naturally; therefore, if a person doesn't, there must be something wrong with them, or perhaps it's an indication that they have a mental health condition.

This argument is obviously weak because although it states that most people naturally conform to gender roles, there is no evidence submitted to justify the argument that if you do not conform to a gender role, then there must be something wrong or you must have a mental health condition.

As you read other people's critical analysis try to be aware of looking for logic and evidence. This will help you to apply these elements to your own critical analytical writing.

Limit the conclusion: do not make recommendations that are inflexible unless they can be defended

Arguments are classed either as deductive or inductive. If you can reach a certain, incontestable conclusion, this is known as a deductive argument. For example, 'If you put your hand into a fire it will burn'. However, most arguments, especially in social work, cannot reach an absolute right or wrong decision. It is likely that you will be working with contradictory pieces of evidence to weigh up and evaluate where there is no certain outcome. This implies an 'inductive' argument where the reasons given lead to a conclusion which is *probably* true. For example, when considering risk in child abuse cases Munro (1999: 18) says:

> Risk assessment instruments, for example, can be invaluable aids but they cannot provide a satisfactory replacement for professional judgement. The statistical problems for predicting rare events combined with the limited knowledge of predictive factors for abuse mean that any instrument used in an actuarial manner will produce an unacceptably high level of inaccuracy.

This quote again emphasizes the need for social workers to present reasoned judgements which are helpful to all professionals who are involved in making complex decisions on behalf of service users.

To limit your conclusion, use language such as *might suggest, indicates* or *increases the likelihood*, rather than *proves, shows* or *definitely*. An example of a conclusion which is limited is, 'Alcohol is highly addictive, therefore if people use alcohol to self-medicate when they are under stress, they are likely to become addicted.'

In this sentence the use of the word *likely* limits the conclusion because it would not be true to say that everyone who uses alcohol to deal with their stress is going to become addicted.

Summary

This chapter has given you a practical guide to critical analytical writing for complex social work cases. Social workers need to use objective, clear and explicit analytic reasoning and they need to be clear about the difference between making reasoned judgements as opposed to being judgemental. However, it can also be argued that their work involves an element of intuitive reasoning. Therefore, understanding complex human interaction empathetically involves the left (analytical) and right (intuitive) brain. Using expert guidance from Munro (1999) and Dyson et al. (2014) the chapter has shown that the organization and analysis of information can have a significant influence on service user outcomes. The chapter made six recommendations about how to do this:

1. Gather information.
2. Check for bias.
3. Select the best information.
4. Identify a main line of reasoning.
5. Explore weaknesses.
6. Limit your conclusion.

By following these steps with your own reports and written arguments you will be able to make strong and convincing arguments on behalf of service users. The chapter argues that social workers need to apply analytical rhetorical skills to information and assumptions in order to find holistic solutions and interventions for service users.

Checklist for critical writing	Yes/No
Does my writing move from descriptive to analytical?	
Will the reader be convinced by what I have written?	
Are my recommendations supported sufficiently by evidence and logic?	
Have I included any unsubstantiated statements?	

Key points

- Writing is part of thinking so the process of writing helps professionals to think analytically.
- Cases in social work are rarely simple. Therefore, analytical writing is required to help to understand how and why things happen as they do.
- Social workers play a vital role in helping other professionals to make complex decisions.
- It is important to be aware of your own assumptions and to check your reasoning to ensure that it is not dependent on assumptions.
- Although there may be constraints on what social workers can write, it is important to fully utilize your professional voice in writing.

Further reading

BASW (2018) PCF 6, https://www.basw.co.uk/professional-development/professional-capabilities-framework-pcf/the-pcf/asye/critical-reflection-and-analysis

Firmin, C. (2020) *Contextual Safeguarding and Child Protection: Rewriting the Rules*, London: Routledge.

Saleebey, D. (2012) *The Strengths Perspective in Social Work Practice*, 6th edition, Boston: Pearson Education.

Thompson, A. (1996) *Critical Reasoning: A Practical Introduction*, London: Routledge.

Wilkins, D. and Boahen, G. (2013) *Critical Analysis Skills for Social Workers*, Maidenhead: Open University Press.

6 Correspondence

Chapter overview

By the end of this chapter you should have an understanding of:

- the professional expectations of correspondence, particularly when used to communicate with service users;
- how to write work emails, letters and memos in a formal and precise way;
- the more flexible approach to using text messages and social media profiles;
- when it is best to use different types of correspondence;
- legal and ethical considerations concerning correspondence.

Introduction

In our personal and work lives we do not function in isolation; we communicate with others daily. Much of this is verbal – face-to-face, on the telephone and, increasingly, on modern media such as video links available through computers, tablets and smart phones. A good deal of communication involves writing – traditional letters, other written messages at work such as memos, emails and types of written communication that blur the lines between formal and informal contact, making electronic connections through texts and social media.

As a social worker you 'correspond' in writing with colleagues, fellow professionals and service users, and your writing, whatever the medium, must be formal, precise and professional. This chapter will therefore explore a variety of written correspondence and examine the skills needed in this aspect of writing. It will also discuss the style and appropriateness of various forms of communication that social workers use to correspond with other professionals and with service users.

Professional expectations of correspondence

We use most if not all the types of communication mentioned above personally to keep in touch with relatives and friends, so it is important to understand what is involved in a professional approach to writing, as discussed more fully in Chapter 3.

Here are some important points to remember. They will ensure that your correspondence is professional:

1. **Be clear about its purpose and audience.** Why are you contacting someone in writing? What response do you expect from them? Be clear and adjust the language in your correspondence with your recipient in mind. Writing to a colleague or fellow professional might be appropriately more intricate than to a service user who you know has limited intellectual capacity or functioning. However, you should not assume that all service users will struggle to understand written communication or that all practitioners will readily understand the content of your writing.
2. **Deal with one issue in each item of correspondence.** Only write about one thing. Correspondence should not involve an agenda of items, as in a meeting. You can address different issues with separate items of correspondence.
3. **Demonstrate empathy.** In keeping with social work professional values, it is possible to show empathy for the recipient in correspondence. You can recognize and share feelings that are being experienced by another person, and you can convey these in writing as well as verbally.
4. **Be succinct.** Use mostly short words, sentences and paragraphs. Correspondence that is plain and to the point will be clearer and more likely to engage the reader.
5. **Make your writing flow with a logical sequence.** It is important that you plan each item of correspondence carefully and consider how it should be written. Correspondence normally starts with a greeting; includes a compliment or pleasantry; clearly states the reason for sending it; requests a response; includes a closing message, and signature.
6. **Use an appropriate style.** All your correspondence should convey a professional social work image. The formal conventions of official letter, memo and email writing include using upper case for the start of sentences and names, and no abbreviations, slang or symbols. This applies to a lesser extent to texts and social media, although this will be explored further below. Use an active voice. Do avoid jargon; all professions have it but it hinders communication with someone not familiar with it. While not being condescending towards service users you should be aware of any reading difficulties some may have, such as English not being their first language, a learning disability or an intellectual impairment, and be prepared to adjust your writing style accordingly. It is best to write as you speak while remaining professional, rather than drift into complex and elaborate language.
7. **Proofread before you send.** Check for errors and mistakes, but also use the above points as a checklist to ensure that your writing is in keeping with the guidance outlined.

Data protection and GDPR

Your organization's confidentiality policies and procedures apply to all forms of correspondence, so you should follow them, bearing in mind what information, including personal details, you commit to writing and who the recipients of your correspondence are.

As outlined in Chapter 1, in May 2018 General Data Protection Regulations (GDPR) came into force. The Government has merged the Data Protection Act 2018 with the requirement of GDPR. Anyone who gives information to an organization has to give permission for it to be kept and used. Service users and carers are entitled through a subject access request (SAR) to see what is written about them. You should always assume that anything you write could be: (1) made accessible to service users and (2) required by a court hearing as evidence.

Having highlighted general implications we now move on to discuss the style and appropriateness of various types of communication that social workers use to correspond with other professionals and with service users, including emails, letters, memos, text messages and online social media profiles.

Emails

Electronic mail was a new concept in the mid-1960s and it is in the last 25 years or so that it has developed and become a regular, global means of communication. Most households now own a computer with email access and this form of communication is an essential part of the workplace. As a social worker, you might agree that the first thing you are likely to do on arriving at your work base is to switch on the computer and check emails. The majority of service users have access to email on computers and, increasingly, on smart phones and mobile devices, able to receive and send them at home.

With each type of correspondence you need to consider carefully when it is appropriate to use it. When is it best to email someone? Letters might be required to convey information of a more permanent nature. Telephone communication involves verbal interaction and is better for an exchange of information that would otherwise result in a string of emails. Emails have tended to replace communication that previously would have involved a letter. They are fast and immediate and can include attachments. You need good word processing skills for them as most social workers write their own emails without admin support.

Various forms of correspondence have, at times unintended, advantages and disadvantages. There may be a temptation to print emails to keep them on file, thus defeating the object of the communication being electronic and sadly rescinding the albeit somewhat unrealistic concept of a 'paperless office'. It is surprising how much paper modern technology can generate. There are professionals who regularly email colleagues who are in the same building and often in the same open-plan room. There is a danger of emails replacing the art of conversation and human verbal interaction.

Email etiquette when using it as part of professional social work differs from the style you might use in personal email messages that you exchange with friends and relatives. It can be easy to fall into an informal style for emails and treat them rather like mobile phone texts. You are writing a formal communication, so it is important that you use correct spelling, grammar and punctuation.

Activity 6.1

Amend the email below from a student social worker to a team colleague, making it more professional.

From: Edward Swales
To: Mary Attah
Subject: earlier today . . .

hi mary

. . . robert called asking for you urgently while I was on Duty. R said his foster son went AWOL on Saturday. They reported him missing to the police over the w/end. R is panicking and wondering what to do as the LAC review is today and wanted ur help pronto if poss seeing you F2F. Told him you would get back to him asap.

Ed

For a suggested more professional version, see appendix, page 150.

When writing an email you should include a subject heading that briefly but clearly conveys what the message is about. The initial greeting should normally be formal (e.g. 'Dear . . .'). The use of a more informal 'Hi' or 'Hello' and greeting recipients by their first name should be reserved for instances when you know them well. A compliment or pleasantry is important, rather than an optional extra, and helps you make a connection with your email recipient.

The convention for signing an email is to use your first name and surname or family name, designation and place of work. Signing using only your first name is to be avoided, unless the email is to someone who knows you well.

There are email facilities to automatically insert an individual signature and agency details in every new message. Email facilities also allow you to set up an 'out of office' automatic reply to let those who email you know when you are away, when you might read it and when they can expect a response. Remember to set correct dates and check that your message is not still being sent when you are back. Receiving an 'out of office' message after the date when you indicate you are away looks unprofessional.

It is very easy with email to add or copy recipients or click 'Reply All' when responding, so it is best not to overuse this. A particular aspect of confidentiality concerning emails is that if names and addresses or other personal information is included in the email or in attachments, you should make sure that all recipients are entitled to see it. It is simple to reply or forward an email that has a string of previous email exchanges as part of it, without noting what has been said before and whether it is appropriate to pass this on to others. Previous messages can be deleted when replying. A message or attachment should not be copied without permission. It is also best not to copy the same email to a mixture of service users and colleagues in an attempt to keep everyone informed. This can result in individuals having access to information where the content or style is not intended for them.

Consider carefully how many people you copy the email to using the 'cc' (short for 'carbon copy') and 'bcc' ('blind carbon copy') facilities. Resist the temptation to include everyone, however tenuously connected with the subject. Do not attach unnecessary files. Although this is a most useful facility, you should not be reckless in its use. In any case, emails are not the best form of correspondence for discussing confidential information.

It is best to keep emails simple, succinct and to the point. They will be much more effective than poorly worded ones. Longer communications or messages are best undertaken through a letter or report. While keeping emails concise, you should make sure that you are including all relevant details or information to make your meaning clear. Ambiguous language or generalities may cause misunderstanding, confusion or unnecessary email exchanges to seek clarification.

It is important to read your email before you send it. Because you can type them hurriedly at your desk, often in the midst of tackling other work, there can be a tendency to disregard formal, clear writing conventions in emails. As you usually have a computer screen and keyboard in front of you at work it might be easier to unthinkingly vent strong feelings, annoyance or sarcasm in emails than in other forms of correspondence. Being able to hastily send a message to an individual recipient, and copy it to others, should not result in a lack of objectivity or courtesy. Emails can convey emotions and can be misinterpreted. In spite of the extra time involved, it is good practice to compose an email, delay responding, and then critically check and proofread it before sending it.

As stated above, social workers have legal duties and powers. Social work agencies and organizations are subject to legal compliance in relevant areas and emails are a legal record of communication. You should be aware of your organization's practice as far as archiving emails, and their storage, retention and retrieval facilities are concerned. SARs under the Data Protection Act 2018 and GDPR regulations arise from a citizen's right of access to personal data that organizations hold about them, including information on email, subject to certain confidential exemptions.

Your organization may have a monitoring system to be notified whenever an alert is raised from sources that may try to access your computer with unnecessary programs. Organizations usually have filter facilities, often called 'spam filters', which are also available on personal computers. These redirect incoming emails to a separate folder if they contain certain unwanted (e.g. obscene) words. Organizations are subject to obscene publications legislation. Even if not reaching this level of legal monitoring, it is unprofessional to send and receive emails containing dubious jokes and questionable humour. Work emails should not be used for personal purposes.

Letters

The traditional letter is less used these days than it once was, particularly for personal purposes. When was the last time you wrote a letter to a relative or friend? There are those who feel we have lost the art of letter writing. However, letters still have an important place in work settings as a more formal method of communication. It can be slower, particularly when compared to email using the derogatory term 'snail mail' or 'smail', relying on conventional postal delivery services. Nevertheless, there are many occasions when in social work it is important, or a requirement, to convey information in writing through a letter. These can range from relatively minor matters, such as confirming an appointment, to making service users aware of decisions that might have a considerable impact on their lives.

Generally formal letters have a conventional layout that include the sender's address and the name and full address of the person you are writing to. Social work organizations will have their own letter-headed paper and modern technology allows this to be available as a document (e.g. Microsoft Word) stored on your computer. Letters should be dated and, as you will normally know the name of the person to whom you are sending the letter, start with the formal greeting ('Dear') using the person's surname or family name. The use of a recipient's first name should be reserved for instances when you know them well. It can be helpful to include a subject heading briefly and clearly stating what the letter is about.

The convention for ending a letter is to use 'Yours sincerely' (or just 'Sincerely') when you have included the name of the recipient. The more formal 'Yours faithfully' is traditionally used when you do not know the name of the person to whom you are sending the letter (and have perhaps started it 'Dear sir or madam'), so it will be rarely used in social work. You should sign the letter and then print your full name under it including your designation and place of work. You might occasionally sign using only your first name when the letter is to someone who knows you well.

The content in the body of the letter can usually be envisaged as a three-part linear development:

1. First paragraph: succinct and to the point stating the purpose of the letter – for example, to give information, to confirm a decision, to make an enquiry, to ask for information or warn someone of consequences (particularly in safeguarding or criminal justice situations).
2. Middle paragraph or paragraphs: outline of relevant information and development of the purpose of the letter in a clear and logical manner. It is important not to deviate or include unrelated matters or 'padding'.
3. Last paragraph: states a logical conclusion and what action you expect the recipient to take, if any. This might include the request for a reply with information by a certain date or confirming that they have received the letter.

A professional letter should be well presented and free of grammatical errors and other mistakes, as well as being clear, objective and courteous. It is part of the image of your organization and integral to the service that you provide to service users. It should communicate an understanding and compassionate approach. Bear in mind who you are sending the letter to and adjust your tone and language appropriately, which should be plain and unadorned in any case.

Use 'you' and an active voice in letters to focus on the reader, particularly service users. As with emails, social workers are usually expected to undertake their own word processing. Occasionally a lawyer from your organization may proofread a letter with legal implications or a court document. Your team manager may scan read all correspondence to check it. However, it is your responsibility to proof-read and check your letters before signing and sending them.

Letters are kept in paper files or electronically as a record of contact and can become part of an audit trail. They can be formally or legally required documents in situations such as an inspection, a serious case review or an enquiry into practice that may have fallen short of expected standards.

Activity 6.2

Here is an appointment letter to a service user using language that is impersonal and dated. Can you make changes to the letter to improve it?

Anytown Social Services
Address
9 May 20XX

Mrs Ada Riley
28 The Avenue
Anytown
Post Code

Dear Mrs Riley

Appointment for 19 May 20XX

Further to our recent contact, please be advised that we have made an appointment to come to see you on the above captioned date at three in the afternoon.

Please note that we will make an assessment of your circumstances and eligibility for services. Kindly have all information such as medical records and evidence of your financial status available.

Enclosed please find a leaflet about community care services. Do not hesitate to contact the writer if you have any queries.

It would help us if you would confirm that the appointment is suitable by telephoning the above number.

Respectfully yours

Linda Holmes Social Worker

For a suggested improved version, see appendix, page 151.

Later life letters

A very specific type of letter is that written by a child's adoption social worker, usually in conjunction with the adopters' social worker, to explain to a child the reasons for their adoption and what led to decisions being made. The letter is written to the child (most commonly toddlers and up to about age 4, less frequently older) who is in an adoptive placement before the adoption becomes final. It is to be read when the young person can understand the issues, usually in adolescence. Although a statutory requirement and containing factual information, the letter will be anything but 'cold' and needs to take account of the emotional impact. It may include giving reasons, for instance, to explain why a child was separated from their siblings.

A good practice guide with suggestions for what should and should not be included (Moffat, 2012) has been published by the British Association for Adoption and Fostering (BAAF). The letter should not be too long, perhaps three or four pages, and it is dated and signed by the social worker. Handed for safekeeping to the adoptive parents, it is good practice for them to have been involved in writing the letter and discussing when and how best to share it with the child. It bridges the gap between a life story book, with a style pitched at the child's current age when it is put together, and the child's placement report (CPR) prepared for the adoption panel, written for adults in a formal way.

Romaine et al. (2007) suggest the letter should include:

- introduction – mentioning the social worker's role and involvement;
- summary of the child's background – details of the birth family and what happened to parents and siblings;
- legal situation – including dates of hearings and orders made;
- family-finding – how decisions were made to find the right adoptive family;
- conclusion – which can include an invitation for the young person to make contact for more information and best wishes for the future.

Although these letters suggest a specialist approach used within a specific service user group, they have implications for other writing and point to transferable skills worth noting. These include:

- the skill of writing personally and sensitively to a specific reader;
- paying attention to tone and language;
- showing empathy and a compassionate approach in writing;
- addressing possible painful issues (that can include abuse, disruption and deaths within the family);
- having responsibility for writing while taking account of the views of others (e.g. the adoptive parents and their social worker).

Memos

Work memos have largely been superseded by emails, but there are times when they may be an appropriate means of, particularly internal, communication. The word *memorandum*, abbreviated to memo, derives from a Latin phrase 'to mention' or 'call to mind', so it is a document or communication that helps one's memory by recording events or information. It can also have a more specific meaning in law as a 'memorandum of understanding or agreement', often between organizations.

Some argue that a memo is a personal note to remind you of something. In July 2014 the US Attorney General had to explain why a memo from an ethics chief criticizing a governor for the manner of handling complaints had only emerged in public after a considerable period of time. Formal requests were made for 'correspondence' between the ethics chief and the governor's office. The Attorney General stated that the memo was not correspondence, it was a document written by the ethics chief and retained by her: 'It did not become correspondence when she gave us a copy 13 months later' (Bluestein, 2014).

Unlike the 'block' style of a letter described above, a so-called 'administrative management style' (AMS) type of writing is more succinct and used for internal memos and situations when you have to be brief and direct. It is intended to inform a group of people about a specific issue, policy or resource and may encourage them to take action. It does not normally use any greeting or closing. The language is formal and if you send it to a number of work colleagues it is a public communication and a form of correspondence. It should state to whom it is sent and who it is from. It includes the date and a subject heading.

Computer software such as Microsoft Word provides memo templates as well as other documents. It is easy then to open a document on your computer, compose a memo and send it to recipients as a hard copy or electronically. It is unlikely that memos would be sent to service users.

Example

MEMO

To: Social workers who are practice educators for university students

From: Amanda Burgess, senior practitioner

Date: 17 July 20XX

Subject: Helpful reading material about working with struggling and failing social work students

I am aware that in the past year, while most students did well in their placements, there were a few that struggled and one failed. Dealing with students that are not showing evidence of their capability in some areas of practice is never easy. We have discussed ways of supporting students and PEs in professional development meetings.

I have come across the resource below that makes for interesting reading. It discusses the stressful and challenging experience of placement supervisors in the UK and in Italy. It highlights the PE's gatekeeping function of preventing unsuitable people from becoming social workers.

I encourage you to read it. I have placed a copy that you can access in the PE resources file of the placements section in the departmental intranet.

Finch, J. and Poletti, A. (2013) 'It's been hell'. Italian and British practice educators' narratives of working with struggling or failing social work students in practice learning settings, *European Journal of Social Work*, 17 (1): 135–50.

Text messages

The Short Message Service (SMS) was used for the first time in December 1992 in the USA when a test engineer sent a short Christmas greeting from a personal computer to the mobile phone of a colleague in another part of the country. In the past 20 years or so text messages have proliferated and become an everyday means of communication between two mobile phones or other devices over a phone network. A texting culture has developed with its own language, abbreviations and text etiquette. It is an established means of communicating and has its own social norms.

Businesses and organizations now use texts as reminders and to confirm arrangements. You may well have received a text from your dentist, car garage or from a delivery firm to remind you of an appointment or tell you that a delivery is on its way. Teachers and university lecturers are increasingly sending information to students, and sometimes to parents, via text, as one of the most reliable ways to ensure that those concerned will get the message.

It makes sense, then, for social workers to consider texting as a valid and effective means of communication. Young people who have grown up within the past 20 years have been called 'digital natives'. Those of us who have been around a while longer are 'digital immigrants'. This may be a reason why text messages seem to be more common among social workers working with young people in children's services, 16+ and adolescent units, and youth offending teams. However, text messaging is by no means confined solely to work with young people. A growing use of technology changes the way in which social work is practised. It is all the more important therefore for social workers to think and act ethically.

Linguist David Crystal engagingly explores the effects of texting on literacy, language and society in his aptly titled book *Txtng: The gr8 db8* (Crystal, 2009). In keeping with these social developments it may help the relationship between a social worker and their service user if the social worker uses a form of communication and language style with which the service user is familiar. A danger is that it blurs the boundary between professional and personal use. We have argued in the forms of written communication explored thus far in this chapter that the language used in various types of correspondence should be formal and conventional. This is difficult with text messages and tends to defeat the purpose of using an informal and readily accessible communication tool. Businesses, on the other hand, tend to send fairly formal messages with minimum abbreviations.

Example

Mrs Patel. Pls remember your dental appt on 07/04/XX, at 10:00, at dentist practice. Pls give 2 working days notice if unable to attend.

Something similar to the above example could well be used by a social worker making an appointment with a service user, of whatever age, who has given consent to this form of contact. Texts are an acceptable way of communicating with service users, only if they agree to receive them.

A young female service user texted her social worker as follows. How should he respond? What are some of the implications involved?

Hi pete! will u be round 2 c me tmoz? enjoyed ur chat so want to talk 2u again. Dont b l8! let me know time. Beth x

The reply might be:

Hi Beth. Glad you found our meeting helpful. I will be here if you drop in to see me at the office @ 3pm tomorrow. See you then. Peter

What implications did you reflect upon in relation to the above example? A social worker is likely to respond in a slightly more formal way while keeping to the tone of a text message. Predictive text facilities in most smart phones mean that the device predicts and adjusts the words while you compose the message. It is common practice for social workers to suggest to service users that they use first names. The social worker would have made initial contact and replied to this text from his work mobile phone. To have used a personal phone would be unacceptable and cross professional boundaries. The work phone, whether used for texts or phone calls, can and should be switched off outside office or agreed working hours. A social worker is not expected to be available to service users 24 hours a day.

Professional ethics would also guide the social worker concerning the relationship he has with a young female service user. There should be an understanding or care plan through which the service user has agreed goals to work towards. Does seeing her on consecutive days fit in with this plan and the goals of intervention? It may be that the social worker and service user had agreed to weekly meetings, in which case the reply would have reminded Beth of this and suggested a meeting next week.

Text messages, particularly those sent from an individual mobile phone, are usually erased from the device after a period of time, so there may be no evidence or verification of contact. You should therefore keep contact records, including whether it was via text, using the systems available in your agency. The importance and purposes of records are discussed in the next chapter.

Think about an instance when a communication you received (email, letter, memo, text) was inappropriate or unclear.

- How did you feel?
- What problems or confusion did it present, and why?
- What did you learn from it about written communication generally and about your own communication style in particular?

Online social media profiles

Even more recent than the texting developments described above has been the expansion of web-based social networks. Individuals, groups and organizations are able to set up a profile with information about themselves and make social links to others through the medium. Facebook, one of the most popular, started as a networking site for universities in the USA in 2004, expanded to the general population, and by 2009 was said to be the largest social networking site in the world. Twitter, allowing users to exchange short 140-character messages called 'tweets', was launched in 2006 and quickly gained worldwide popularity. 'Tweet-ing' is now a recognized verb. The networks link with each other so it is possible to tweet messages that also appear on the sender's Facebook profile.

Organizations, including government agencies and charities, promote them-selves by inviting individuals to 'like us' on Facebook or 'follow us' on Twitter. A prominent accountancy and business advisory firm produced a publication for local government entitled *From Housing and Litter to Facebook and Twitter: Updating your status* (BDO LLP, 2012), advising local authorities on the use of social media. A subsequent textbook explores *Social Media in Social Work Edu-cation* (Westwood, 2014), outlining instances of social media being used for teaching and learning with implications for the development of social work skills. Cooner (2014) examines the use of social work students' engagement with Face-book as part of an enquiry-based blended learning design of a module about fam-ilies as systems. These are reminders of ways in which the World Wide Web has transformed the exchange of information and how activities possible through the internet have become part of the human psyche.

Social media developments include the sharing of images and photographs on Flickr, Pinterest, Tumblr, Instagram and other regularly emerging new platforms. Video clips are shared on YouTube and similar media. Blogging online – sharing thoughts and ideas through text, photos and video – is an increasing form of com-munication. Council websites and those of other organizations, including social work agencies and universities, now have links to these facilities for the public to obtain more information and news about them and provide feedback.

It is clear that the ways in which service users communicate and interact with service providers are developing and changing. Many social workers will have their own Facebook, Twitter and other accounts and might refer to their work while networking with friends. There are ethical considerations here. Essex County Council dismissed a social worker in May 2013 following comments on her Facebook page describing three children being placed in care as a 'career high', and saying a judge had given the parents a 'rollicking' (BBC, 2013). This highlights the need for caution about what you publicly disclose regarding your job as a social worker in your social media profile and how you phrase any com-ments. It is important not to cross personal and professional boundaries even in situations when you are not 'on duty'. Recruiters and employers are increasingly using search engines to find background data on candidates and employees.

As with a mobile phone, it would be unacceptable and cross professional boundaries to allow a service user access to your personal social media profile. However, as a social worker you may work for an agency or project that has a social media profile and it would be proper to make comments and join in discussions concerning service users' and carers' participation and involvement. Such interaction should be in keeping with social work values to respect people who use services and safeguard their individual confidentiality. There are dangers relating to sharing information and data that might be held and available or accessible about social workers, as well as service users.

A social worker with a particular role that is shared with professionals from other disciplines, e.g. best interest assessor, or approved mental health professional (AMHP), might create a private Facebook discussion group and invite fellow professionals to join. They can exchange information, discuss training experiences and gain new perspectives. Another social worker might engage with service users by creating a Twitter account under a user name that reflects a professional title. This could be for a service user group with a common interest such as young carers, parents of children with behaviour difficulties, or people experiencing mental health problems. The social worker might post general information relating to practice issues, targeting areas of relevance to the service users, making it clear that the facility could not address confidential personal or individual issues. While these uses of social media seem acceptable, provided social workers keep to ethical guidelines, one can think of examples that must clearly be avoided. It would be unacceptable and unprofessional for a social worker to post personal photos and those of colleagues on Facebook. Posting particular service user-related pictures, even if not showing their face, about an outing or groupwork for instance, would be improper, particularly if there is no attempt to hide their identity and personal details.

Part of safeguarding children and vulnerable adults includes digital safeguarding. You should be aware of privacy settings not only in relation to social media but also regarding all forms of computer-based communication, including emails, Facebook Messenger, WhatsApp and other constantly evolving facilities. Professionalism includes ethical use of technology – being aware of and checking your privacy settings and permissions, not using public storages for private information, keeping your own email address and phone number private, using end-to-end encryption facilities and secure passwords. Modern technology has made it easier for those who maliciously use social networking to obtain confidential information. Sadly, such 'hacking' has become increasingly prevalent. One private residential social work facility known to the writers had to deal with the consequences of a service user being an expert hacker.

Various social work regulators publish professional standards for social workers that include acting safely and with professional integrity. Examples of these are those published by Social Work England (2019). They include standards stating that:

> As a social worker, I will not . . . 5.2 Behave in a way that would bring into question my suitability to work as a social worker while at work, or outside of work . . . [and] 5.6 Use technology, social media or other forms of electronic communication unlawfully, unethically, or in a way that brings the profession into disrepute.

SWE Professional Standards Guidance addresses confidentiality and includes the reminder that:

Confidentiality also applies to the use of technology and social media. Social workers should not make reference to anyone they support or disclose personal or professional information about colleagues, managers, or employers on social media, an online forum or blog. Even if the references are anonymised, the identity of the person may be recognisable to others.

(SWE, 2020)

Activity 6.3

The following exercises are adapted from Amy Wiggins, Careers Adviser, University of Kent.

First impressions

It is said that your first impression is not made with a firm handshake – it is with a Google search. Try to Google your name and find out what a colleague or service user could discover about you. Don't forget to check Google images too. What did you find? Do you have a presence on Google? If so, what are the positive and negative representations of you? Is there any information available which you consider inaccurate or misleading? Fill in the table below with your thoughts.

Positive	Negative	Inaccurate

Social network check-up

Do you have Facebook, Twitter, LinkedIn or a presence on another social network? What image are you portraying there? Look at your pages and answer the following questions. Put **N/A** for any questions that do not apply to you. Answer **Y** for yes or **N** for no.

Ask yourself . . .	Facebook	Twitter	LinkedIn	Other (please specify)
Would I be willing to read my last five status updates/tweets at an interview?				

Ask yourself . . .	Facebook	Twitter	LinkedIn	Other (please specify)
Would my current profile picture give a good impression of me to an employer?				
On my public profile (accessible by everyone, even if they are not connected to me), have I said anything that others may deem offensive? (e.g. swearing, politically incorrect 'jokes', racism, sexism, homophobia, rudeness)				
Am I connected to any groups that others may find offensive?				
Can members of the public see photographs I have been tagged in?				
Would employers be able to see inappropriate photographs of me? (May include drink, drugs, inappropriate clothing, swearing)				
Have I said anything negative about my work/university on my page?				
Would an employer be able to see the skills and experience I have from my page?				

You can help reduce the amount colleagues and service users can see about you by altering your privacy settings, but you cannot always rely on this – you need to remember who your contacts are.

Moving forward

Hopefully by now you will have a clear idea of your online presence. Please make a note below to review what you have found, and what further action you may be taking.

1. Evaluation – how do you feel about the information or images colleagues and service users can currently see about you?
2. Are there any changes you will make to your online presence as a result of completing the audit? If so, what will these changes be?

Summary

This chapter has proposed that all correspondence used by social workers to communicate with service users must be undertaken professionally. This includes a formal, clear and precise approach to writing emails, letters and memos. The chapter discussed more recent developments concerning the use of text messages and social media profiles. It suggested that it is right for social work to keep up to date with modern media but that it is also important to be aware of the difference between personal and professional boundaries when using such types of correspondence.

A consideration highlighted by the chapter was to decide when it is best to use different types of correspondence depending on their purpose and the needs of service users with whom we are communicating. Legal and ethical considerations were also discussed with a reminder that correspondence can form part of a record of contact with service users that may be inspected or needed for reviews and enquiries.

Key points

- You should approach all types of correspondence that you use to communicate with service users in a professional manner.
- The work emails, letters and memos that you write as a social worker must be formal and precise but also clear and user-friendly.
- Your use of text messages and social media profiles can be more informal and flexible but you must not cross professional boundaries.
- You can use the most appropriate type of correspondence for different situations and service users.
- You should be aware of the legal and ethical considerations concerning all forms of correspondence.

Further reading

Hood, J. (2013) *How to Book of Writing Skills: Words at Work – Letters, email reports, resumes, job applications, plain English*, Magill, South Australia: WordCraft Global.

Jackson, R. (2019) *Social Media and Social Service Workers*, Glasgow: Iriss, www.iriss.org.uk/resources/insights/social-media-and-social-service-workers

Sparks, S. (2011) *Manager's Guide to Business Writing*, 2nd edition, Madison, WI: McGraw-Hill Professional.

7 Records

Chapter overview

By the end of this chapter you should have an understanding of:

- the importance of record-keeping as an essential part of social work practice;
- the purpose of records and how they apply to different audiences;
- ways of writing records to a professional standard;
- the importance of taking into account legislation that entitles service users to have access to their records;
- implications for writing different types of records.

Introduction

The crucial importance of maintaining records to a professional standard in social work is strikingly highlighted by the case of a senior social worker who was struck off as a result of poor record-keeping. A senior social worker in Hertfordshire was informed by a school that a girl had bruising on her thigh and had passed pink-coloured urine. He stated that he thought the school would include the information in a report and he did not record it. He also failed to record or to inform a manager that a child was not at home when he visited. His records suggested all was well. There were other instances of this practitioner failing to report concerns and not keeping adequate case records. He admitted finding it difficult to balance involvement with service users and recording. The then social work regulator, the General Social Care Council (GSCC), at a disciplinary hearing, concluded that the social worker should be removed from the register as he had put vulnerable children in his care at risk of harm. The case made headlines in the social work press such as *Community Care* (McGregor, 2010).

Reflection

- What is your reaction to the practice of this social worker?
- What issues and implications emerge for you from the above information?
- What can you do to avoid getting into such a situation yourself?

This is an extreme and fortunately not a frequent example. Your initial reaction might be very critical of such a worker. But who of us can say with certainty that we would not cut record-keeping corners to some extent when under pressure and faced with a high workload? The example is a reminder that keeping records is crucial and an essential professional activity in social work. The details outlined, albeit brief, highlight issues such as:

- the need to fully record significant information;
- sharing information with other agencies;
- ethical practice and accurate recording;
- accepting the importance of recording;
- integrating record-keeping as part of your workload.

If you are a social worker, in whatever sector or setting, no matter what service user group you are working with, you will be required to keep records. These could well be extensive and take up a good deal of your time. You may feel that relating in face-to-face contact with service users, rather than sitting at your computer, is why you became a social worker and you may resent the time you have to spend writing records. However, meaningful paper (or computer) work is and always has been an intrinsic aspect of good practice. 'Bureaucracy' that leads to rigid procedures and where the volume of writing impedes effective action is not good for social work, however devoting the time necessary to produce robust records is indispensable. This chapter will explore how keeping a clear record of what you have done is an essential part of your work.

The following are examples of capabilities and professional standards that apply to social work in England but, as previously stated, are echoed in the expectations and requirements of regulators and frameworks of other UK countries and further afield. The PCF *intervention and skills* domain includes the requirement that social workers must demonstrate the capability to:

... maintain accurate, comprehensible, succinct and timely records and reports in accordance with applicable legislation, protocols and guidelines, to support professional judgement and organisational responsibilities.

(BASW, 2018)

One of the key points of SWE Standard 3, *Be accountable for the quality of my practice and the decisions I make* requires you to:

3.11 Maintain clear, legible and up to date records, documenting how I arrive at my decisions.

(SWE, 2019)

Records are a form of written communication, so they require professional and technically correct writing, as discussed in previous chapters. Remember that through your records you are also communicating with others. It is appropriate in relation to records, therefore, to consider who you are communicating with and why. Who is the audience for your record-keeping? What is the purpose of records in social work? Let us look at these two questions in turn.

Who are records for?

Your records are part of and help to support your own effective professional practice. Regularly reviewing them enables you to build a picture of your involvement with a service user, detecting themes, raising concerns and noting developments and progress, or lack of it, over time. Records help you arrive at considered judgements and aid your decision-making. However, there is a danger that you might treat records as merely your own observations, as you might do with your notes of lectures and seminars or training sessions. You must always bear in mind that you are also keeping a record of your work that others will have access to, so your records must reflect all potential audiences, as is the case with all your professional writing.

You are writing for your social work agency or organization. You will need to follow the organization's protocols, policies and procedures and use required formats and systems. Increasingly within social work the practice is to keep electronic, computer-based records. Agency records are formal documents that will need to be checked or inspected.

Your writing is also for your colleagues. Records normally belong to a team as well as to the organization and there will be fellow professionals and support staff who have access to them. If someone else looks at your records they should find no ambiguity. Your records should be intelligible to others and give the person reading them a clear account of your contact with service users.

As outlined in Chapter 1, legislation gives service users and carers a right to read what is written about them. Would they appreciate what you have written about them? Service users and carers may not be pleased with what you have written because they do not agree with a professional judgement that you have recorded, but as they are an important part of your audience and the records are about them, how you word what you record and the accuracy of it are considerations that must guide your writing.

Other professionals may also need to have information that you have recorded. These can include medical and health, education, youth and community work, criminal justice, housing and other local authority professionals, police, psychologists, social care and voluntary organization workers and many more. Although some will be social work professional colleagues, the majority will read what you have written having had different training, being used to different terminology and belonging to a different professional culture. As a consequence, your records must be clear, accurate and precisely written in a way that avoids misunderstandings. It would be wrong and unprofessional if you used records as a platform to air professional differences of opinion.

What is the point of writing records?

There are a number of valid purposes for keeping records. Nonetheless, a challenging initial question you can ask yourself is, 'Should I commit this to writing?' Records are permanent; they can be added to but not erased. So what you record must be necessary, relevant and written in keeping with social work professional values such as respect for service users and carers, being non-judgemental and avoiding prejudice and discrimination for any reason.

That said, keeping a record of work is important for you and for the organization. You may use your records in professional supervision to discuss your work, reflect on your practice, test hypotheses and plan for the future. Your records can help you review and evaluate your work; they are essential for informed decision-making. Records can build a picture of your involvement with service users and carers and are part of the assessment–planning–intervention–review and evaluation social work process. They may also provide data for research. When you record a meeting with a service user at the office, some other venue or a home visit you are making a note of:

- the purpose of the interaction;
- its outcome.

Records also provide an organization with evidence about the work undertaken by its workers. They may be a source of statistical data that can be collected and contribute towards the achievement of performance indicators. They are an official record of the agency's responsibility for and response to service users and carers. Records are essential if evidence is needed in court or if there is a serious case review. The organization needs to have a record of contact with service users and carers and of information shared with other agencies.

As an example, the serious case review overview report prepared by Hester Ormiston, an independent author for the Bolton Safeguarding Children Board, into the death of a child, confirms that:

The report has used electronic social work records of case notes, emails, contact records, initial assessment and strategy discussions, as well as paper and electronic records from two Children's Centres:

- IT records of registration and attendance
- The registration form
- Records from the crèche
- Multi Agency Resource Panel (MARP) referral and panel minutes

(Ormiston, 2013)

What is recorded can provide information to check facts retrospectively and may highlight shortfalls or lack of services. This can help planning. Records will stay on file for years or decades. Although the policies of different agencies vary, routine records of referrals, initial assessments, advice giving and signposting to other organizations are likely to be kept for a period of some five years. Records of assessment, planning and social work intervention may be kept for up to 35 years. Records of substantial and significant involvement, such as in child protection, are usually kept for 70 to 75 years. The responsibility you have for what you include in records and how you write them is noteworthy when you consider the length of time that the information will be kept within a record system. Service users may request to see their records years after their contact with social workers.

Records are a legal safeguard if there should be litigation or a formal inquiry into work standards. Unfortunately, due to tragedies and investigations when social workers are criticized for shortcomings there has been a tendency in recent years to see recording as a means of 'covering your own back' so that you or your organization cannot be blamed later for something you have done incorrectly or for something you have not done. Making this the main purpose for it results in defensive recording. A blame culture encourages the identification of someone culpable, a scapegoat, when things go wrong. This is an unfortunate and negative view of recording when it should be seen positively as evidence of professional accountability.

Example

A social worker in a child protection team included this entry in a 'contact record'.

(Date)
Home visit done. Child seen.

Do you see this as an example of a succinct record, token note-keeping or in some other way? A social worker may record the minimal information needed to provide evidence for performance indicators or as a future safeguard to show that contact with service users took place. However, such a short record does not contribute to a picture of involvement or address assessment or intervention goals. It does not make a note of the worker's professional judgement relating to that visit. Records should relate to the PCF holistic capabilities and interdependent domains.

Records can be used as a means of information sharing with others. An important reason for keeping accurate and up to date records is that colleagues can refer to them when you are not there. If a duty officer or another colleague deals with a telephone or personal call from a service user or carer with whom you are currently working, they will benefit from looking up your records and responding to the person in a way that fits with the assessment, plans, goals and outline of involvement that you have recorded.

Example

The record written by a mental health social worker after visiting a service user referred by her GP was as follows.

Visited Mrs Ramsay late afternoon to assess her current situation causing her some distress. She was very cautious and mistrustful. Personal history suggests she has been managing well on her own until five or six days ago. Now experiencing what appears to be a manic episode, highly verbal and rather repetitive. Describing impulsive behaviour. Displaying disjointed and erratic thought patterns, suspicious of friends and relatives attempting to help her. Offered to refer her for medication and to investigate possible admission to a mental health unit, which she said she would accept.

When a relative made telephone contact later that day because the service user's condition was deteriorating, she got through to an out of hours duty officer who was able to access the social worker's record on the computer and advise that the service user be taken to the local hospital's A&E department to be seen by a psychiatrist on call. The duty officer undertook to pass on the social worker's assessment to the hospital.

This example shows the importance of recording immediately as part of good practice and to provide the best service possible, even when the time of day or working hours may prevent the ideal immediate response in certain instances.

When a worker leaves or hands over work to someone else for other reasons, records provide continuity and the means for another worker to start their contact in an informed way. When there is a fresh referral it is good practice to check records in the system to see whether the person or family are known to the organization and, if so, what work was previously undertaken and when.

Another purpose of records relates to the need to share information with other professionals. Formal inquiries into tragedies have routinely highlighted poor communication and lack of collaboration and information sharing between agencies. Factors contributing to poor inter-agency partnerships include the number of organizations that may be involved, differences in the training of various practitioners, their values and their professional ethos. Effective 'team working' within multidisciplinary teams and as part of interprofessional collaboration (Martin, 2013) is not achieved without conscious effort. The information that needs to be shared is contained in records of contact, chronologies and minutes of meetings, so it can be a great help if these are written and kept in a way that can be jointly used when appropriate. It is also vital to record joint decisions arrived at through pooling the information available to various agencies.

An essential purpose of records is the organization's and your professional commitment to service user and carer participation and how their views and wishes are taken into account when working with them. Records allow you to give an account of how you involved service users and carers in providing information and making decisions, allowing their voice to be heard in terms of how they were consulted and how they participated in the work you undertook with them. The commitment to service users and carers is an important reason for keeping records and should influence what is recorded and how it is worded, which is what we now move on to consider.

What and how to write

We have already noted the need for clarity and avoiding misunderstandings. Earlier in this chapter there is an example of very brief recording resulting in minimal information, which is of little use. Conversely there is a danger, either due to 'playing it safe' or because of your style of writing, of including too much descriptive detail. Records are a summary of work undertaken so should be succinct yet comprehensive with no unexplained, significant gaps. It is worth considering what is relevant to record and what might be irrelevant details that you can leave out. Subheadings can help. The level of significance of the information that you are recording is a good measure to help you decide what to record. Safeguarding concerns *must* be recorded. Descriptions of conversations or who said what and when could be summarized or omitted.

Activity 7.1

Read through the case note example below and summarize it to make it a more professional record. Aim to include relevant information and disregard irrelevant details. Using subheadings might help.

H/V to Aina Akinjide

When I arrived Mrs Aina Akinjide answered the door and she took me into the dining room but also showed me her bedroom. She pointed out many ornaments and photographs, especially of her late husband. We sat in the dining room and we talked. At one point Aina made afternoon tea so we then sat at a large dining room table and she offered me chocolate biscuits that she had received from her daughter as a Christmas present, with which we had with a cup of tea. She said she was keeping quite well. She enjoys watching TV in the evenings and some during the day.

Aina talked a lot about her family, pointing at photographs. She also showed me her cat Fluffy that she likes a lot. Fluffy sits on a blanket on the settee next to Aina while she strokes him. She said she was very happy with how things were going. She has regular visitors from her church where she goes on Sundays. Someone comes to collect her and gives her a lift. She manages to cook snacks for herself and also has frozen meals delivered, most of which she likes. There are one or two she is not so keen on. She goes to a local day centre on Thursday afternoons between 2:00 and 5:00 pm where she chats to friends and sometimes does some arts and crafts. She is doing a scrapbook with photos, pictures, newspaper cuttings, pressed flowers and some artwork.

I thanked Aina for the afternoon tea and told her to contact me if she had any queries. I said I would in any case call again in three months.

For a suggested more professional version, see appendix, page 151.

Case notes can say a good deal about you. You may portray your interests and what you feel strongly about. It is important to remember that you are a professional practitioner writing professional records that are most effective if they remain focused on an agreed action plan. You should ensure you include no personal bias. Bearing in mind their various audiences, records go beyond notes that you are making for yourself as a worker so the language you use is important. It is helpful to avoid jargon and abbreviations. Local authorities use a system code for types of abuse, for instance, but referring only to the code, which can in any case change over the years, will make your record of little if any meaning to someone not familiar with it. Chapter 2 has suggestions for avoiding jargon.

Activity 7.2

Which of the following statements seem the most factual to you? Which appear to rely on opinion for all or part of the statement?

1. I smelled alcohol on his breath.
2. He is an alcoholic.
3. He attends AA meetings.
4. He told me he attends AA as regularly as he can.
5. He was unsteady on his feet and he seemed drunk.
6. I noticed a number of empty bottles of wine and beer in the kitchen.

For suggested answers, see appendix, page 152.

Fact vs. opinion. Being judgemental vs. making professional judgements

As well as avoiding jargon, it is also helpful to write in plain English, avoiding complex language. You need to consider carefully how you are going to phrase what you record. Records are a means of providing mainly factual information. You should not include views based on your personal beliefs and interpretations, and the tone you use should not be alarmist, condemnatory or disapproving. There is a difference between being judgemental and making professional judgements. Records should be non-judgemental. Professional judgements, including raising concerns, must be acknowledged and be evidence-based. When recording a home visit, for instance, a factual description of the place, which might be dirty, cluttered and unkempt, is acceptable, particularly if you describe the conditions. Opinions such as the occupants being 'too lazy to clean', 'messy' or living in 'disgusting conditions' have no place in professional recording.

When using the organization's formats and systems, recording may feel like filling in a form, not allowing you much if any scope to paint a picture of your contact with service users and carers (see Figure 7.1). Electronic, computer-based records may help you by including instructions and making clear the details that have to be recorded in required places. They can also constrain you by at times providing drop-down menus with a limited number of choices and having limits to what you can record due to the size of a file or even the number of characters that the system allows to be included in a particular field. When you follow given protocols a skill you need to develop is to use the required electronic system within its parameters and functions but avoid being formulaic and repetitive, and learn to use the system in a way that can still give an accurate account of a service user's needs, circumstances and involvement with them as a person.

Your name:		Main ID:			Completed by:	

Background Information and referral details   **Confidential**

Can be collected directly from the person or from someone else on their behalf

Family name		Given name		Title	
Preferred name		Date of birth		Age	
NHS number		Social care ID			
Gender		Preferred language			
Ethnicity		Marital status			
Religion		Sexual orientation			
Current address		Employment status			
	Postcode:	Current phone number			
		Mobile phone number			
Permanent address (if different)		Email address			
		Accommodation type			
	Postcode:	Housing type			
Lives with		Accommodation tenure			

Referral details (If self-referral address will be assumed to be as above. If in hospital identify person's ward.)

Referral date		Referral time		Location of referral	
Referral method				Referral type	
Referrer name				Referrer role	

Reason for referral (identify reason type right then detail)	
Details	

Contact assessment

To be completed with the person and/or advocate on the person's behalf

Your main current difficulties and concerns (including perceived impact on life and relevant personal history)

Details

Have there been any important recent events or changes in your life?	Yes		No	

Details

How you would like your situation to improve?

Details

Figure 7.1 Adaptation of Functional Analysis of Care Environments (FACE) form

Legislation

In Chapter 1, we pointed out that the Data Protection Act 2018 and GDPR entitles service users and carers to access their personal records upon request. *Your Rights: The Liberty Guide to Human Rights* includes a section about social work records. It highlights possible exemptions, for example, 'A parent would not normally be entitled to see a child's records without the child's consent. If the child is too young to consent, the parent can apply on the child's behalf.' Another example given is that:

> a parent who is accused of child abuse is unlikely to be given access to the child's records, or to information provided by the child but recorded on the parent's file. But the parent should be able to see other information recorded about him or herself, such as the notes of an interview or home visit, so long as disclosure would not expose the child to risk or prejudice law enforcement.
>
> (Addis and Morrow, 2005: 89)

It is usual practice for a social worker to be present when a service user is given access to their personal records and to arrange for the exercise to be conducted in a sensitive way. The file and other information will probably have been prepared in advance. Data about someone else in the person's file and anything that might identify an individual who has provided information about the service user will normally be exempt and removed.

The relevant legislation provides a reminder that when writing you should bear in mind that service users and carers may read what you have recorded about them. Your writing about service users and carers must be in keeping with social work professional values.

Record-keeping checklist

- Learn about the record-keeping system in your organization.
- Abide by your organization's policies and procedures for record-keeping.
- Write when the interaction you are recording is as fresh as possible in your mind.
- Make some notes at the time of a meeting or home visit, either longhand or with an electronic device such as a laptop or tablet.
- Subheadings may help you order your thoughts after an event (e.g. when you get to the office after a home visit). These might include:
  - the purpose of the meeting;
  - the context of ongoing intervention/contact;
  - service user's needs/circumstances;
  - your professional opinion/judgement;
  - the service user's views;
  - your factual observations;
  - any concerns;
  - outcome/agreed action points.

- Be clear, accurate and precise.
- Avoid unnecessary descriptive detail.
- Record significant information in a comprehensive way, yet succinctly and to the point.
- Avoid jargon and shorthand phrases that others may not understand.
- Ensure your records are intelligible to others.
- Clarify who you are referring to when mentioning people (e.g. Mrs Agarwal, maternal aunt, etc.).
- Include professional judgements but do not be judgemental or prejudiced.
- Avoid derogatory or emotive language and views that are disrespectful.
- Record all contact, including telephone calls, emails and texts. Avoid any gaps.
- Focus on the action or care plan.

Types of records

Different local authorities and social work organizations will use diverse systems for recording and refer to various records by different names. It is impossible therefore to give a comprehensive list of them or to offer guidance in relation to specific local procedures. Employers should provide induction and on the job training relating to their recording practices and expectations.

It may be helpful nevertheless to reflect on some of the most usual types of recording that you are likely to come across as a social worker.

Case records or case notes

Agencies will keep a record of the service users with whom they have had or currently have contact. The record will show whether the individual or family have an allocated social worker – whether the case is 'live' or 'closed'. Case records should include the correct personal information to identify the service user, family or carer. These records often include summaries of assessment, plans and work undertaken that provide a picture of the involvement that the organization has with the service user and the service user's current circumstances. They may include information such as details about a service user's income and savings at a specific point in time, as service users may have to pay for or contribute towards services provided for them.

Case records can be a source of reference, information and accountability. The information recorded, stored in a computer system and/or kept in a file is a record of the service user's story during the time that social workers have been working with that person, including their family or carers if relevant. It should help anyone reading the record understand what has happened in the service user's life at specific points in time.

The term 'case' in this and other contexts is arguably contentious. Most individuals would probably prefer not to be referred to as a 'case'. Each one of us is a person in our own right with our own feelings, wishes and aspirations. Some organizations may apply another name such as 'social work record' but the term has traditionally been used by social workers to refer to how many 'cases' they have allocated to them, their case load, case studies and case management. What is important when you are writing 'case records' or 'case notes' is to remember that they refer to an individual person who shares a common humanity with you.

Contact or running records

Many of the features described in the section above apply also to ongoing records that social work agencies keep to note each time the service user has some contact with the service. This will include home visits, meetings at the agency or another venue, telephone calls, emails, texts, letters and any other form of interaction. In most organizations these records are kept and accessed electronically on computer systems. Some organizations, particularly local authorities, may still have a book in which social workers write longhand notes during, or immediately after, an interview or visit. If the individual social worker is the only person with access to those notes it questions their usefulness given the audiences and purpose of records discussed earlier in this chapter. If you make such notes at the time of interaction with service users it would seem appropriate to then transfer them to a record system that can be accessed by others.

Contact or running records chronicle every point of personal, electronic or written interaction with a service user, each one dated, thus providing a record of the frequency of contact. They may be a part or a section of a larger 'case record'. A skill you will need when writing them is to be able to summarize, keep them short and be succinct while giving the gist of the contact. Where possible, particularly when you are recording face-to-face interaction, it is good practice to note the purpose of the contact and its outcome.

Day and residential work records

In social work and social care establishments, such as day centres and residential homes or units, some form of contact record will be kept but these may take a somewhat different form as the interaction with the service user can be continuous for long periods of time and for 24 hours a day in residential care. There may be a logbook or incident record to note significant events and interactions with any one of a number of staff on duty. Each service user should also have their own personal individual record. The previously mentioned serious case review overview report prepared for the Bolton Safeguarding Children Board into the death of a child makes suggestions arising from examining the records from two children's centres providing a universal service to parents from the community:

- Staff should be trained to ensure that registration details are completed more fully or with explanations for any gaps.
- The signing in sheet should note if the person attending is registered or not (registration is not required to attend).
- The service should consider the development of a brief record for each session, noting the title, learning for the parents, and which adults and children were present.

- The referral process for MARP (Multi Agency Risk Assessment Panel) should be reviewed to ensure a CAF (Common Assessment Framework) is completed if more than one agency is in contact with the family.

(Ormiston 2013)

Day and residential centres are required to keep medication records and administration sheets. Establishments also have staff handover documents that help workers when they take over a shift to have relevant information about significant issues that may have impacted on the behaviour or wellbeing of service users. It is more common in some day and residential settings to have hand-written books or record files. Required skills when writing these include accuracy of information and legibility, relevance and clarity.

Care plans

A care plan is a written agreement between the service user, social worker and any other relevant persons. It should be based on the views of all concerned. It will record how to meet needs identified in assessment and should include SMART (specific, measurable, attainable, realistic and timely) goals. It will list support needed, who to contact if necessary and how. Care plans vary for different service user groups and settings but may involve planning for care needs, health, education, personal development, strengthening networks of support and/or relationships, along with support for a service user at home or the planning of placements in residential or foster care.

Most organizations provide care plan forms with headings and sections to complete. Unfortunately many of these are not user-friendly either for the service user or the social worker. Within these limitations your writing needs to be clear and formal but personal. You can use the service user's own words and phrases and you should avoid jargon. Service users may write their own plan if they wish to do so, or parts of it, and they should sign it. They must feel that they have agreed the plan and that they 'own' it. The plan should indicate when it will be reviewed.

Specific agencies will have different types of care plans including mental health care plans, carers' support plans, direct payments plans and looked-after children care plans.

Action plans

A care plan can lead to a separate recorded plan of action, or an action plan may be part of it. It should include objectives to work towards and clear outcomes in relevant aspects of a service user's life. It will list actions and responsibilities, what has been agreed, who is responsible and when. An action plan can focus on a service user's strengths. It can include crisis and contingency plans outlining actions to take in an emergency or to meet unforeseen events.

Although many organizations have their own documentation it is best for an action plan to be in a format and style that the service user is comfortable with. They should be person-centred. The action can address relevant stages of a person's life currently and in the future.

Support plans

Many organizations will subsume these as part of care and action plans. Whether this is so or whether they form separate plans, they should also be outcome-focused and person-centred. It can be effective to write them as if in the service user's own voice, using the first person.

Carers may require their own support plan following the assessment of a service user and of the carer's capacity to care, their mental and physical health needs, and their employment and leisure needs.

Chronologies

A chronology is a succinct factual recording of significant events and changes in circumstances listed in ascending date order – earliest date first. This skeleton of key incidents provides a sequential story of historical information concerning a service user and, where relevant, their family. It is a good tool to share with other professionals, showing patterns, indicating progress or lack of it, identifying crisis points, risks and levels of concern. It is good practice to have a chronology as part of the records of every service user and it can be used to inform the decision-making process. A chronology summarizes what can appear to be too much information to take in and make sense of within a full recording system. It contributes to assessment, planning and review. Some local authorities now have computer systems that allow you to click on a 'significant incident' facility that automatically transfers that information from general records into a chronology. However, even when using such a system your skill is to summarize the entry into a brief outline of key points.

Chronologies have traditionally been undertaken in children's services, particularly for child protection, although an adult safeguarding chronology is a tool that is becoming increasingly used. The usefulness of having a timeline of significant incidents providing a profile of a person or family is valid for any service user group. Initially a chronology is prepared based on the records held by one agency. However, sharing information with other organizations at meetings and through discussions results in a multi-agency chronology of events. This can highlight weaknesses and strengths, 'filling in blanks' when there are gaps in knowledge; assumptions that may have been made; disguised compliance; positive sharing of information and ensuring all concerned have a full picture.

Formal inquiries into tragedies and serious case reviews have promoted the importance of chronologies for service users where warnings can be missed or dismissed and agencies have been criticized for inadequate chronological recording and poor communication and information sharing. Pemberton (2010), writing in *Community Care*, proposes that a clear chronology of events in safeguarding cases can show agencies where risks lie. However, she highlights social workers' experience that it can be hard to find the time to do them. She outlines how key events revealed a pattern of risk in the serious case review undertaken by Birmingham Safeguarding Children Board into the death of 7-year-old Khyra Ishaq, identified as 'Case Number 14' at the time of the review in July 2010.

Example

Summarized extracts from the chronology in a serious case review (Pemberton, 2010). The chronology included in the serious case review on the death of Khyra Ishaq revealed a pattern not apparent to disparate agencies.

2 May 2001:	*Khyra Ishaq born.*
15 December 2005:	*Khyra and sibling fail to attend a child development appointment. This was one of several cancelled appointments. Information was not shared.*
1 March 2006:	*Pattern of defaulted appointments emerging.*
28 February 2007:	*Health visitor makes a referral to children's services following reports from Khyra's mother that the father is abusive.*
20 March 2007:	*Mother meets school to discuss concerns that Khyra had been stealing food. School agreed a behaviour support manager would observe Khyra. Information was not shared.*
6 December 2007:	*Mother tells teachers Khyra will be home-schooled.*
19 December 2007:	*Deputy head of Khyra's school contacts social services. She and a colleague do a home visit but are refused entry.*
19 December 2007:	*Child protection referral made by deputy head, but delays occur due to staff capacity. Later, two teachers visit Khyra's home. Mother refuses them entry.*
28 January 2008:	*Education social worker (ESW) visits Khyra's home. There is no answer. Deputy head also contacts children's services for the third time regarding concerns.*
30 January 2008:	*ESW calls children's services following a home visit. Social services suggest a common assessment framework, which ESW records was inappropriate due to mother's resistant attitude to professionals.*
8 February 2008:	*An ESW and council mentor visit Khyra's home. They do not see Khyra.*
21 February 2008:	*Two social workers on a prearranged visit are refused entry to Khyra's house. Khyra and some of her siblings are brought to the door and the social workers report they have no concerns for the children's well-being.*
17 May 2008:	*Khyra pronounced dead at Birmingham Children's Hospital, from an infection caused by starvation.*

Minutes

Minutes of meetings are a record of the purpose of the meeting, when it took place, who was present, issues discussed, decisions taken and agreed actions. There are times when admin support staff will take minutes but as a social worker you would do well to develop the skill yourself. Such minutes may be of a particular meeting with service users, with other professionals or a team meeting at work. An indication of good teamworking can be that social workers within the work group agree to share the responsibility for chairing and taking the minutes of team meetings.

In common with other forms of recording already explored in this chapter, one of the key skills of a minute-taker involves summarizing the event and discussion, avoiding unnecessary detail. Agenda items should be clearly indicated and linked to decisions relating to them, what was accomplished and action points to take forward. It is important to record who agreed to undertake the action. In a meeting with service users there may not be a formal agenda, so as a minute-taker you would clearly identify and list issues discussed as if they were agenda items.

As a minute-taker you should be as neutral as possible. Facts rather than feelings should be recorded. If the meeting considered a report or other written material, there is no need to write any of its detail in the minutes. Every person attending a meeting, and others who sent apologies or who need to be kept informed, should receive a copy of the minutes as soon as possible. Being quick in this respect not only avoids forgetting certain parts of the meeting that you are recording but it also gives those who have agreed to take action an early reminder to do so.

Summary

This chapter has stressed the importance of keeping social work records and the need to integrate the activity into your work rather than regard it as a tedious chore. We noted that you write records for your own practice, your agency, colleagues, other professionals and service users and carers. The chapter highlighted that records should be written with the service user in mind, since legislation entitles them access to their records and being person-centred is in keeping with professional social work values. The chapter reviewed the types of records used by various organizations and explored ways of writing them to a high professional standard.

Key points

- You should regard record-keeping as important and an essential part of social work practice.
- You should bear in mind the audiences for your records and why you are writing them – their purpose.
- You need to develop skills in writing records to a professional standard, including the ability to write records as factual summaries of work undertaken and to justify professional judgements.
- Legislation entitles service users to see their records and gives them rights in keeping with professional social work values.
- It is helpful to know how to adjust your writing style to different types of records.

Further reading

Prince, K. (1996) *Boring Records? Communication, Speech and Writing in Social Work*, London: Jessica Kingsley.
SCIE (2019) *Social Work Recording*, London: Social Care Institute for Excellence.

8 Reports

Chapter overview

By the end of this chapter you should have an understanding of:

- the importance of structure and style in professional reports;
- how to describe, analyse and evaluate information in a report;
- how to adjust your writing to different types of reports commonly used in social work.

Introduction

Reports are a core feature of social work; they are used in a wide variety of situations from court reports to care assessments. At the most basic level, once it has been established *who* the report is for, a report needs to do three things:

1. It must describe briefly *what* it is about.
2. It must address the reasons *why* something has happened.
3. It usually has some recommendations or conclusions that state the impact (*so what?*) of the information.

Reports are always written for a purpose. Having this in mind will help you to stay focused when writing. They are read for factual information so that work can continue in a seamless manner or decision-making can take place. The need for clear reports is especially important in multi-agency settings, which are now the norm in social work. Therefore, ensuring the use of accessible language is a good starting point for any professional report writing. The content of any report must be based on research and be factual, objective, detailed and concise.

This chapter starts by outlining the structure and style necessary in professional report writing. It then analyses the stages of typical reports, from a description of what happened, to analysis of why it happened and then evaluation leading to evidence-based recommendations. Three types of social work report are examined in detail (case reviews, assessments and progress reports). Finally, an example case report is presented with exercises so that you can apply your learning from this chapter.

Consider the audience for your reports

Similar to all forms of writing, it is vital that you consider carefully the audience for your reports. Reports are informative and often make recommendations, so it is important to think about who you are informing and what they need to know. This will help you to ensure that your reports are focused and relevant. The four questions in Activity 8.1 will help you to do this.

Activity 8.1

For each of the following reports identify:

- Who is the audience?
- Why is the report required?
- What do the recipients need to know?
- How will the report be used?

1. A court report on a young offender's progress in establishing meaningful structure to their life.
2. A report to the local housing association on the lack of meaningful social activities available to young people on a large estate.
3. A report to a school on the various care arrangements that have been put in place for a young person during the past five years.

For suggested answers, see appendix, page 152.

Structure and style in professional reports

Reports in any area of professional practice are tightly structured documents; they are often designed to be read by a number of different professionals, so having a clear structure makes them easier to read. Readers often want to get to certain parts of information fast, such as the methods, or recommendations. This is why the structure is so important. If you ask a manager what makes a good report they are likely to tell you it must be short and accessible. Reports are usually read on a 'need-to-know' basis rather than from cover to cover, therefore headings and sections are useful. The structure of a report depends on what it is about and who it is for; some can be very simple and only need a few lines of information, others are wide ranging and detailed.

Think for example of the Munro Report (2011), which has been one of the most influential reports on children's services and beyond. Most people who have read it will have paid particular attention to the recommendations because it is a working document and this is the information that readers really need to know for their own practice. However, the rest of the report is useful as it sets the context, explains how the information was gathered and gives detailed studies of particular cases.

Generic structure of a report

Although later in this chapter specific types of report are considered, the generic structure for a report will usually include the following aspects:

1. Introduction.
2. Context: brief description of events.
3. Methods or procedures.
4. Analysis of why things occurred in the way that they did.
5. Recommendations or conclusions.

Often reports are divided by headed sections. Therefore, as a writing technique it is sometimes useful to turn each heading into a question (this can be deleted later). The effect of this is that it enables you to focus directly on the need-to-know information of each section. For example:

- Context becomes: What happened?
- Methods becomes: What did I do?
- Analysis becomes: How can I make sense of this?
- Recommendations becomes: Based on the evidence presented, what might help?

Writing style in reports

If you are new to an organization it is always helpful to read some reports written by more established colleagues so that you get a feel for the type of report and style of writing that is expected from you. In general your writing style for reports needs to be clear, concise, accessible and objective. You will need to make points clearly and support them with evidence or examples. It is also helpful to arrange the points that you make in a logical order – either a hierarchy with the most important points first, or a chronology so the reader can see the sequence of events. To make your reports easy to read, use the first sentence of every paragraph to state clearly what the paragraph is about and make sure that each section relates directly to the heading above it.

One of the difficulties of writing is knowing how much information to assume; in general write as if the reader has similar basic knowledge and experience as you, but has not been involved in this case at all. Professionals who read many reports as part of their job emphasize that the elements which make a good report are that it:

- is short;
- is in plain language;
- is well researched;
- sets out options clearly;
- makes strong and supported recommendations;
- can be used as ammunition to support a case.

(Williams, 1995)

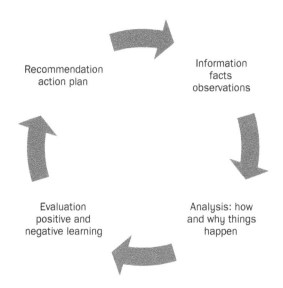

Figure 8.1 The reflective learning cycle (Kolb, 1984)

Reflective writing in reports

All well-written reports will be reflective in their nature. This means that through your writing you have been able to:

- step back from the situation and see it clearly;
- show that you are self-aware about your practice and how you are perceived by others;
- see things from a range of perspectives;
- apply your theoretical knowledge to a practical social work setting.

Reflective learning (see Figure 8.1) is often visualized as a cycle:

- The cycle starts with descriptive writing which should be kept to a minimum and only used to describe events and observations which are critical for the audience to understand the situation.
- Next is analytical writing, which tackles *why* and *how* things have happened in the way that they have.
- Evaluative looks at the positive and negative elements of a situation in order to make an informed judgement.
- Finally, recommendations are made which should be SMART:
  - **Specific:** are your recommendations well defined? Try to avoid setting unclear or vague recommendations, instead be as precise as possible.
  - **Measurable:** be clear about how you will know when your recommendations have been achieved. Using dates, times and amounts is one way to represent measurable recommendations.

○ **Attainable:** making impossible recommendations will only end in disappointment, so you should try to make the recommendations you set challenging, but realistic.

○ **Relevant:** try to step back and get an overview of the case/service user: relationships, work, education, finances, etc. Consider how relevant each recommendation is to the overall picture.

○ **Time bound:** set a time scale for the completion of each recommendation. Even if this is reviewed and revised it will help to retain focus.

Activity 8.2

Use the reflective learning cycle to improve your own report writing.

1. Describe your own report writing experience up to now.
2. Consider how your report writing compares with other forms of writing you do, and why you find report writing challenging.
3. Reflect on the strengths and weaknesses of your reports (if you have had feedback on your reports think about that).
4. Write a set of recommendations for yourself to improve your reports (if possible share this with a colleague or supervisor).

Using charts and diagrams

One aspect of reports which is emphasized by people who read them a lot is that they must enable readers to get to the important information quickly. Sometimes information is easier to access in a chart or graph rather than within standard paragraphs. For example, if you want to plot change over time it may be easier to show this in a graph, or if you want to show the percentage of something it may be easier in a pie chart. There are many charts, tables and diagrams available in Microsoft Word. When you are writing your own reports try to bear this in mind and assess the right format for the information you are presenting. In addition to this, try to make sure that you explain in words any data from charts and analyse it.

Describing, analysing and evaluating information in a report

Describing information

When you are describing people or events for a report you need to be as factual and objective as possible. Therefore, it is important to try to ensure that none of your own biases come into the writing. It is also important that this section of a report is as brief as it can be while still covering the key information. Try to think about what readers will really need to know and:

- order your notes into a logical sequence;
- distinguish between what is fact and what is opinion and your own subconscious bias.

Analysing information

This is the section of a report where you can stand back from the facts and information presented and try to make sense of it. You will need to think about the positive and negative information that you are presenting and draw on your experience as a social worker to try to understand why things have happened as they have.

It is useful at this point to think through some of the theoretical approaches to social work which you studied as a student to see if this helps you to make sense of the current situation. It is also useful to remember that the way that social workers analyse information may be different to the way that other professionals view the same information. For example, you may employ the 'social model' to understand someone's mental health whereas a health professional is more likely to use the 'medical model'. This does not mean that one is right and the other is wrong, but it does mean that you will need to have an awareness of other perspectives if you are to fully understand why things have happened in the way that they have.

Often asking hypothetical questions about the situation helps you to see it from other perspectives and putting yourself in the shoes of the service user or another professional may help you to understand their actions or perspective. In order to do this you will need to:

- Try to be objective by standing back from the information and observing it critically. Wilkins and Boahen (2013) have written helpfully about this.
- Use your professional knowledge and experience to help you understand the situation.

Here are some examples of hypothetical questions that may help you to analyse information.

- What would have happened if . . . ?
- If I were in a similar situation, how would I feel?
- If this situation changes in the future, what is the likely impact on X?
- What recommendations can be made based on the evidence?
- From the perspective of X (another professional), how might this be interpreted?

Evaluating options

Most reports are written so that decisions about what to do next can be made. It is your role to evaluate the information which you present and make a range of recommendations based on that. To evaluate information you will need to ask questions such as: What can be learned from these facts and events? What might be done differently next time? What advice can be given?

Types of report commonly used in social work

Although all reports have common features such as formal structure and professional style, there are many different types of report. This section identifies three types which are commonly used in social work and describes them in detail.

Case review reports

Case review reports (e.g. for a review meeting or case conference) need to be factual and provide an accurate account of events. It is important for the information presented in this type of report to be unbiased and objective. Case notes or reports act as a working document which will be read by other colleagues who may need to pick up on work that you have started, or intervene on behalf of the service user in a particular way. The sections in this type of report usually include:

- a brief description of the facts;
- the person(s) involved – names, roles in the family/relationships;
- the sequence of events – a simple account of events;
- the action taken – a list of actions taken in chronological order;
- the cause and effect – explanation of the outcomes and impact of the actions taken.

Assessment reports

Another important type of report which social workers often work on is an assessment report, which comes about as a result of one or more interviews or conversations with a service user (and their family/carer). Assessment reports need to be well structured and comprehensive, but this framework should also be flexible enough to allow for 'organic conversation' to develop as well so that you can build a rapport with the service user and so that the process does not feel mechanical. The sections in this type of report usually include:

- information about the service user – name, age, etc.;
- physical health – first impression of appearance, speech and health;
- mental health – is there a history of mental health issues, or any signs that this may be an issue;
- personal circumstances – family background, domestic situation and social networks;
- other factors – work, education, finances.

When writing up an assessment interview there is often a structured form to complete, which is now expected to be typed and held online for ease of reading and accessibility for other colleagues who may need the information. It is important to write up the assessment interview while it is still fresh in your mind and before other information clouds it.

Assessment reports may also go a little deeper into the service user's capabilities. For example, perhaps the assessment report is about an older person who has had a period in hospital after a fall, but wants to return home to live independently. In this situation the social worker will need to evaluate the older person's independent living skills and make recommendations about an appropriate care package to put in place so that the service user is supported to live independently. In this case further information is needed, such as:

- facts about the service user (see all sections above);
- information on what the service user is *able* to do;
- information on what the service user is *willing* to do (their disposition and motivation);
- areas in which support is needed;
- recommendations.

Progress reports

A third type of report which social workers often write can be categorized as a progress report. These may be needed in circumstances such as a court report to account for the progress a service user has been making in turning their life away from crime. This type of report requires the social worker to check on the progress of a service user at regular intervals and focus on certain activities or criteria as a measure of progress. This may involve looking at engagement with education, training or work, or participation in community groups and support networks. Progress reports are often used to make extremely important decisions about service users' lives – for example, whether to recommend a custodial sentence or to allow a child to reside with a parent. Therefore, the information in the report must be clear, accurate, unambiguous and unbiased. It will also need to make comparisons between one period and another, identify any changes and give reasons for their underlying causes and effects. The sections in this type of report usually include:

- introductory information – name, age, etc.;
- period of time covered by the report;
- positive developments – causes and effects;
- negative developments – causes and effects;
- direction of progress;
- recommendations based on evidence.

Activity 8.3

Below is a transcribed report from the criminal justice system. It has been reproduced almost exactly except for identifying details that have been anonymized and spelling/grammar errors corrected so that they do not distract. Afterwards there are several exercises to help you to practise your report writing skills.

Rewrite the offence description, cutting out any subjective information and rewording anything to make it flow better.

Offence description

X's recall of the theft was given to the police during interview on [date]. X informed the police on this occasion that he had seen the telescope in a neighbouring garden and planned to take it when it was dark. X did this, taking the telescope to his own garden. This took place between [date and date]. However, I found it hard to believe that a young person of five foot would be able to carry such a large item over a wall and back into his garden and I informed X that I suspected that he had help. X, like most young people, felt that to tell about any others' involvement is 'grassing' and maintained that he carried out the theft on his own.

X did however on the second interview give information which has been passed on to police in regard to the involvement of an adult male of 21 years. This indicates that X is beginning to understand that everyone has to take responsibility for their behaviour and that friends do not allow others to take responsibility for their behaviour.

X's offending behaviour has historically included thefts, handling stolen goods, assault against the person and non-domestic burglary. Over the past year X has not committed any violent crime which indicates that he is beginning to manage his emotions much more appropriately.

For a suggested answer, see appendix, page 153.

Activity 8.4

Analysing information into logical order and making it precise. The offender assessment presented here is quite muddled. Use your analytical skills to write a timeline showing the important events in X's life. Try to cut out any extraneous information so that it is 50 per cent shorter than the original.

Offender assessment

a) *X is a young person of 13, but he has already been involved in criminal activities before being considered legally responsible at 10 years old. X received a referral order at 10 years old for setting fire to his mother's letter box following a row and a threat from her to sell his motor bike.*

b) *From the age of 5 X has been known to social services and he has a history of problematic behaviours and parental mismanagement of these. His name was placed on the child protection register prior to* youth offending team involvement from [date], which resulted in the local authority applying for a full care order which X is currently subject to following a long period in secure accommodation on welfare grounds.

c) Although on a full care order, X resides with his mother and older brother and more recently his mother's partner (known to probation services). His relationship with his mother remains difficult, but they are fully supported by social services and X receives daily support from them including the provision of education.

d) Prior to this, X was not attending school, and had been excluded due to behaviour difficulties from a very early age. At age 7 he was permanently excluded from school. He is subject to a statement of Special Educational Needs and he has been assessed as academically much below his chronological age. X has been assessed by a speech and language therapist as having expressive and receptive language delay. This means that he has problems with both communicating and understanding what is being communicated to him. He has also been assessed as having attachment disorder, as a result of his early traumatic experiences.

e) He suffered abuse from an early age through domestic violence and an extreme significant trauma at the age of 6. This extreme significant trauma on an already traumatized child resulted in further disruptive, compulsive and reckless behaviour.

f) At the age of 11 and following much professional input X was made subject to a secure accommodation order due to his increasing impulsive and reckless behaviour.

g) Since his secure accommodation order expired, X's transition to the community has been, in the main, successful. Although X still requires firm but fair boundaries and daily 1:1 input. X's impaired emotional development gives way to very limited problem-solving skills and he is unable to deal with and manage his emotions. He acts impulsively when overwhelmed by his emotions and can at times reject those close to him and it is at these times that he is at risk of further offending. Like all children, X tests boundaries which remain problematic in regards to his mother's ability to maintain boundaries and support X's development. Like many parents, his mother will give in to X for an easy life and at times she mistakenly colludes with her son believing this to be a sign of love. All of this said, X's mother does not try to blame others and she willingly accepts the support provided to her and her son. More importantly she continues to stand by her son when many parents may have given up.

h) X is currently subject to a supervision order, this is with six months at a special school and a three-month curfew order. X worked well with the order despite reoffending in the very last week of the intensive *supervision and surveillance programme (ISSP). Given the issues which X has, he has still made progress.*

i) *Two years ago X was unable to discuss any issues with professionals, nor was he able to be part of a group without being verbally abusive and threatening. In situations where he is anxious X used to have a bad stammer. Now X's stammer is minimal even when he is anxious and he is able to discuss issues in a more mature manner, although he still has moments when he is overwhelmed and will disengage. He is also making progress within a group setting.*

j) *X's initial response to all the options in the pre-sentence report (PSR) was to completely disengage from education and activities. However, after discussion with myself and the social worker he has now settled and he has since fully complied with the day care programme [school's name], he has attended school without absence and his mum has reported that his behaviour at home has improved. X has been informed that his motivation and compliance is evidence that he should be given a community-based order, although he is aware that he may still get a custodial sentence.*

For a suggested timeline, see appendix, page 153.

Activity 8.5

This offence analysis is difficult to read. Can you arrange these offences in a graph so that they have better visual impact?

Offence analysis
In looking at his offences, X committed five offences in 2006 (non-domestic burglary × 1, public order × 1, criminal damage × 1, violence against the person × 1 and theft and handling stolen goods × 1). In 2007 X committed five crimes (theft × 1, non-domestic burglary × 1, theft and handling stolen goods × 1, violence against the person × 2). In 2008 X committed three offences of theft and handling stolen goods. This year X has committed three offences of theft and handling stolen goods and non-domestic burglary. X's offending has decreased in regards to violence and may signify that he is maturing and beginning to manage his feelings more appropriately.

For a suggested answer, see appendix, page 153.

Activity 8.6

This recommendation does not state what a positive order might be. Use the evidence you have read above to make a recommendation to the court.

The court requested that all options were considered in this report. I have, with all professionals involved, looked at the positives of each of the orders available both in terms of X and his continued progress and protection of the public.

The court could make X subject to a detention and training order, however at this time and given the progress X has made it would, in my opinion, not be of benefit in the long term while it may give short relief to the police and community. A detention and training order is also likely to increase X's criminal peer group and thus would, in my opinion, be counterproductive.

For a suggested answer see appendix, page 154.

Editing, proofreading and checking

As this chapter has established, reports are important documents. Therefore, it is vital to allow time to edit before submitting any report. When you are editing consider whether you have fulfilled the brief, and completed all of the sections adequately. Think about whether anything could be deleted; look particularly for waffle, redundant words and repetition (try to be as economical as you can be with your language). Streamline your language using short sentences and precise vocabulary (see section on plain English in Chapter 2). Proofread all of your reports before you submit them as this will help to eliminate errors and ensure that the reader is not distracted by mistakes and your writing is clear. Proofreading is often easier said than done, as it can be difficult to spot your own mistakes, however you will get better at it with practice. There are some key things to help you proofread:

1. Print out the document which you are proofreading because errors are easier to spot on the page than on the screen.
2. Read the report aloud to 'listen' for mistakes.
3. Look out for common errors such as those mentioned in Chapters 2, 3 and 4 (sentence structure, tenses, punctation).
4. Don't just rely on Word to correct your spelling and grammar mistakes because this often gets it wrong.

Use the following checklist before you submit your reports.

Question	Tick
Have you responded directly to the reasons why the report was requested?	
Does the report answer questions which its readers may have?	
Is the information you provided in the appropriate sections?	
Have you checked the accuracy of all of the information?	
Have you analysed the information that you provided?	
Are the recommendations you make supported by the evidence which you provided?	
Have you removed all irrelevant information?	
Is it written in an appropriate style (formal and jargon free)?	
Have you proofread it carefully?	

Summary

Written reports are a vital aspect of professional social work. After writing a report it is good practice to reflect on your learning as a professional and as a writer. Try to reflect on the most efficient techniques for gathering and recording information. Think about how you select information for inclusion or exclusion and how you use the evidence that you gather to make convincing recommendations on behalf of the service user.

As you become more experienced as a social worker your reports will become more strategic and focused on the information which you know from experience is needed, and with continued feedback and practice you will also develop your 'professional voice'. Remember that the key elements in any report are:

- Who is it for?
- What is it about?
- Why have things happened in this way?
- So what is the impact?

A postscript on jargon

The writing skills of social workers hit the headlines in August 2015, reinforcing the need to avoid jargon in court reports, to consider who the report is written for and what is involved in developing a 'professional voice'. Judge Jeremy Lea was quoted criticizing a social worker's report on a woman who wanted to care for two children. By using phrases including 'imbued with ambivalence', 'having many commonalities emanating from their histories', 'issues had a significant interplay on (her) ability' and 'I asked her to convey a narrative', the judge felt that the social worker had made the meaning of her report inaccessible to the service users involved in the case.

The judge was quoted in *The Independent* ('Judge criticizes social worker over report which "might just as well have been written in a foreign language"', Monday 03 August 2015) as follows:

> 'Reports by experts are not written solely for the benefit of other professionals, the advocates and the judge. The parents and other litigants need to understand what is being said and why.'

> He added: 'There were passages . . . which were written in language which made their meaning quite opaque. I suspect as far as (the woman) was concerned, these passages might just as well have been written in a foreign language.'

The judge highlights perfectly our own view; that social workers need to write reports with all audiences in mind, in accessible language, with clarity, precision and the use of plain English. We hope this chapter has helped to reinforce those principles.

Key points

- Reports need structure and formal expression.
- Reports require reflective and analytical thinking and writing.
- Reports are working documents which are used for making difficult decisions.

Further reading

Bogg, D. (2012) *Report Writing*, Maidenhead: Open University Press.
Watt, J. (2012) *Report Writing for Social Workers*, London: Sage/Learning Matters.
Williams, K. (1995) *Writing Reports*, Oxford: Oxford Centre for Staff Development.

q Funding applications

Chapter overview

By the end of this chapter you should have an understanding of:

- the use of persuasion in writing to seek funding for aspects of your work;
- the implications for writing to obtain funding within your agency;
- effective ways of applying for additional funds for service users;
- writing funding applications for specific projects.

Introduction

As a social worker everything you do is likely to involve some writing. When talking to a service user face-to-face or on the telephone you might make notes, perhaps at the time, certainly shortly afterwards. If you are at your desk, you will almost certainly be writing on your computer, or perhaps longhand. Writing is involved in the social work process of assessment–planning–intervention–review and evaluation. As you think and plan it is useful to jot down ideas and timelines. If you are in a meeting, making relevant notes can help you focus and participate.

Previous chapters have already explored different types of professional writing in social work and specific tasks that involve written communication. This chapter introduces another set of responsibilities that may face you at some point – making a case to persuade others to fund an aspect of your work. The service provision or care package that you are planning may require you to apply for funding within your agency. There may be instances when you seek to obtain extra funds for your service users from a body external to your organization, such as a charity or trust. Your work may develop in a way that you consider applying to a funding body for a specific project or research. Some of the principles involved in different types of funding applications are similar but we will review them separately below. You may think it unlikely that you will at some point have to write a funding application, or that you will ever be required to do so, but in a socio-political climate where central government funding is restricted and local budgets are limited you may be finding yourself increasingly involved in this form of writing.

We have in earlier chapters already considered the importance of preparation, planning and organizing your writing. We noted the importance of writing professionally with the appropriate style and tone to address your audience and how crucial it is to write in a way that is grammatically correct, coherent and to the point. All these involve relevant skills that are transferable to putting together funding applications. A key additional characteristic of the writing discussed in this chapter is *persuasion*. In Chapter 3 there is a section on persuasive writing that you might benefit from looking at again. In this chapter we will explore how, through your writing, you will be seeking to persuade someone that they should commit funds to the cause for which you are applying. Through your writing you will be conveying information and putting forward a reasoned and persuasive argument so that those responsible for allocating funds will be persuaded that what you are suggesting is desirable and meets their funding criteria.

Seeking funding within your agency

Providing social work services costs money. Local authorities and other social work agencies work to finite budgets that may well be frozen or cut in times of austerity. There have from time to time been suggestions such as each social worker being allocated an individual budget to administer, but this seems to be no more than a speculative idea. A 2014 survey of an 'average day' in social work provided interesting insights into how social workers spend their time and what their concerns are. One social worker commenting on the impact of financial cuts on social work practice stated:

> Following a reassessment of a person's care a support plan is written, if the support plan is over budget it has to go to a panel of management and is usually 'knocked back' so a lot of work is spent sorting this out.
>
> (Unison, 2014)

In most organizations, team managers are allocated a modest budget amount, which they are able to authorize. This is likely to be a sum of not more than a few hundred pounds. Beyond this social workers routinely have to apply for funding, perhaps to a service manager with responsibility for agreeing higher amounts or typically to a panel consisting of service managers and probably someone at director level when substantial financial support is involved. Panels may include other members, such as representatives from a local authority's commissioning, contracting and finance departments.

To make a case to a panel you are likely to submit an assessment of the service user's need, a care plan, a realistic indication of costs involved and a written panel application. Some authorities may require you to attend the panel meeting and make a verbal submission. You will therefore also need presentation skills involving clarity, putting forward a case that is coherent, realistic and to the point. An experienced social worker likened it to being on the *Dragons' Den* TV programme in which budding entrepreneurs make a pitch to millionaire 'dragons' and attempt to convince them to invest in their business ideas. A professionally written proposal including relevant issues and a persuasive line of reasoning will underpin your application for funding and help your presentation by focusing on key points.

It is important for you to get to know the system, who are members of the panel and how it operates. Make sure you understand the criteria used for decisions. You need to do your homework before writing any funding applications. Even though your organization may have set amounts agreed for certain types of provision – for example, a 'personal educational allowance' of, say, £500 for looked-after children – its expenditure may not be automatic and you would have to give acceptable reasons for spending it in a particular way, such as special lessons for a child. Your agency is likely to have a funding request form, which may include a commissioning referral. You are responsible for your own practice. If you have made an assessment that it is appropriate to provide a particular service, then you should follow the process through, irrespective of whether you think that you will be successful or not.

The Government has published *Care and Support Statutory Guidance* relating to the Care Act 2014. Section 10.85 states:

> Due regard should be taken to the use of approval panels in both the timeliness and bureaucracy of the planning and sign-off process. In some cases, panels may be an appropriate governance mechanism to sign-off large or unique personal budget allocations and/or plans. Where used, panels should be appropriately skilled and trained, and local authorities should refrain from creating or using panels that seek to amend planning decisions, micro-manage the planning process or are in place purely for financial reasons.
>
> (DoHSC, 2020)

There is a danger of being deterred from making a panel application because 'it involves too much work', 'my manager is against it', or 'panels care more about keeping to budget than agreeing objective assessments'. You may feel under pressure not to seek extra financial resources. However, you have to remind yourself that the duty to advocate on behalf of a service user is an important aspect of your role as a social worker. If at first you are not successful, your panel may have an appeal process or you can recommend that a service user can complain to a Local Government Ombudsman.

In completing the application paperwork, your writing will need to include background information about the service user, details of the care and support plan, services involved, and goals and outcomes to be achieved. Specify what work you will undertake. It is important to accurately provide all the information required. Some of it will be brief and factual. However, the funding request form is likely to have headings that allow you to expand and make a persuasive case for the particular service, placement or care package. Explain your rationale and how what you are proposing will meet the service user's needs. It is important to avoid jargon and awkward 'shorthand'. Remember that you are writing about a vulnerable person.

Activity 9.1

One of the headings in the 'Health' section of a local authority form is 'Mobility'. Below is an entry with jargon and awkward 'shorthand' phrases. Reword it to make it more reader-friendly.

MOBILITY: The client is able to mobilize short distances with physical support of two people at all times. Mobility and movements are quite slow and she is unsteady on her feet. The client is unable to initiate use of walking aid due to increased confusion. Due to the above presentation, the client is at high risk of falls.

For a suggested answer, see appendix, page 154.

The form you are completing may have several sections in which you could insert similar information to that shown above. These can include 'Background', 'Risks', 'Care currently being provided', 'Health and social care needs', 'Summary', etc. It is important to think carefully about what you will write in each section, avoid repetition and ensure the case you are making through the form flows to a logical conclusion. The quality of your writing can make the difference between a panel agreeing to or refusing your application. You should avoid unsubstantiated general statements such as 'this person needs residential care'.

Example

An application for residential care had the following assessment summary.

Mrs A is a 78-year-old lady who lives alone in a semi-detached house that she owns. She has a diagnosis of Alzheimer's disease and has no awareness of time and space. She does not recognize family members. Due to Mrs A's increased confusion and cognitive decline she is unable to plan, organize or initiate tasks, which places her at a high level of risk without ongoing support and supervision. Mrs A is quite anxious and needs constant reassurance, especially at night time. Her daughter stays overnight in order to support her mother, as Mrs A wakes up to five or six times asking for a drink or needing reassurance.

Concentrate on key issues and how what you are requesting meets eligibility criteria. You might argue that there could eventually be a need for services that would cost more in the long term if funding is not agreed at this stage for the measures you are proposing. It may be necessary for you to go back to review meetings to justify the expenditure. You can refer to previous information in an application.

> **Example**
>
> *B's memory and ability to undertake tasks has deteriorated since the last carer's assessment. The memory clinic reviews B regularly. This can be evidenced in the last report produced by X, memory service nurse specialist, which is uploaded on to our system under 'Health reports'.*

You may explain the impact on a carer to support an application for an increased care package or residential care.

> **Example**
>
> *C explained that her husband follows her everywhere in the house, even when she goes to the toilet. In the evenings particularly he may repeatedly ask to go home or where his mother is. She likened this to a 'dripping tap' and says she feels 'suffocated'. C acknowledged that she sometimes becomes so tense and stressed that she shouts at her husband, who reacts by being verbally aggressive towards her. She describes the emotions that she feels at these times as ranging from frustration to anger and guilt.*

Reflection

- To what extent do you think 'painting a picture' of the pressures on the carer using her own words gives a true account of her situation?
- Does it enhance the application, or make it less professional?
- Would the carer accept the wording as suggested?

In an application you will need to outline details such as hours of care or costs, which should be realistic and detailed. You may be required to use a resource allocation tool or provide a costs breakdown. It is important to specify how you will know that goals have been achieved, showing that the original plan was justified and thus money has been well spent.

Obtaining external funds for service users

In the course of your work you may assess a need that you cannot meet within the budget available for your service provision or through government funds and benefits to which service users are entitled. This could be for something like a holiday for an individual or a family, other outings, or equipment or household appliances for service users on low incomes.

The focus of this chapter is on the skills involved in writing funding applications. However, it is important to also develop the skills and knowledge involved in keeping up to date with information. You need to gather particulars regarding government policies and practices about statutory sources and benefits, and where to find information. It is helpful to build a database of charities, funds or grant-giving trusts relevant to the service user group with whom you are working, noting who is eligible and how often you can apply.

You should recognize the value of, and aid access to, independent advocacy. Although you will be using skills in writing applications to obtain funds, it is good practice to do so in close liaison with your service users. Many charities request that the claimant themselves must make an application, so you will probably be enabling and supporting service users to complete an application form. Some charities may request a letter of application or will have facilities to apply online. Service users may have to set up an account online with the charity. Applications usually include personal details, including income, questions to ascertain eligibility, social and health needs, and an agreement to accept the charity's terms and conditions.

On the other hand, some charities specify that individuals or families cannot make direct contact – the request has to come from a professional such as a social worker or be sponsored by a professional. The application may be for a looked-after child with foster carers who do not have the confidence to apply themselves. Your role in this instance will also be as an *enabler* and you will be using your writing skills to support them.

The organization that you are contacting will have a specific application procedure, so many of the points made earlier in this chapter regarding internal applications apply here as well. Full, accurate and well-presented information is again important. The request is likely to be for one event (a holiday, outing) or equipment (disability aid, appliance). A service user's diagnosis or declared disability may be relevant. Explain the purpose of the request and how it will benefit the person or family, or the difference it will make. You can include your own professional opinion. Ensure you are asking for something within the organization's remit and that it meets their criteria to make a financial grant. You should be asking for money for something that is not available through a statutory source. Put the request in the context of services that you are providing and show how it will enhance the quality of life of the service user.

Examples

I am applying for a bespoke sports wheelchair so that X can pursue his ambition to join a local wheelchair basketball team.

This application is for an iPad so that Y's parents can introduce more fun ways to interact with Y to enable him to communicate.

In making a case for service users' needs to be met through financial support you may feel that to obtain the funding you have to paint as 'negative' a picture as possible about their disability, social need, emotional state or general pressures on them. You might be faced with the ethical dilemma of highlighting service users' disadvantages and limitations to get money. This may also be the case when you are helping service users make an application for government benefits, such as Disability Living Allowance. While it is true that you will be attempting to make the strongest case to obtain funds, what you say must not be exaggerated or disrespectful. Physical, emotional and social needs can vary and be more acute at some times than others. So in your application you may emphasize instances that show when the individual or family are in greatest need.

You must not ignore the importance of a covering letter, which you are likely to write last. We have already noted in Chapter 6 that good professional letters are well presented, correctly worded, clear, objective and courteous. They represent you and your agency and can assure credibility. Your letter introducing a funding application may make the difference between it being read and considered or rejected, thus falling at the first hurdle. A bad initial impression is difficult to overcome later. It is best to address the letter to a specific person. As with all effective letters, the opening paragraph should state its purpose – succinctly outlining what the application is about. A middle paragraph or paragraphs summarize what the funding is for – how what you are asking for will benefit the service user. Avoid merely duplicating what is in the application. The end paragraph states what action you expect the recipient to take – to give your application favourable consideration and let you have the result as soon as practicable.

Projects and other proposals

You may feel as an individual social worker that there is not a lot you can contribute to service development, research and evaluation. However, there are many occasions when you can use an innovative approach, think outside the box, and through collaborative working achieve change, reach desired outcomes and improve services.

This may lead you to identify projects to work on, which will involve writing skills. You will need to communicate, at least through email, with project partners. You will also need to identify and write down project aims based on areas of improvement that you have identified, involving people who use services and carers.

The Social Care Institute for Excellence (SCIE) published a guide to practice development based on collaborative working in social care (SCIE, 2010). It encourages individuals and groups to come together to improve areas of practice. The improvement focus methodology includes these points:

- Decide, with input from front-line workers and those using the service, which aspect of work you would like to change or improve. Here are some examples:
  - improving safeguarding through better identification of risk at the point of assessment;
  - improving signposting to people not deemed eligible for social care services (e.g. self-funders);

  ○ improving responses to carers' needs as identified in assessment.

- Ensure that all participants, including commissioners and service providers, have an agreed understanding of the definitions in the subject area – provide written definitions. For example, improving 'outcomes' would require a definition of the term such as: a good outcome is one identified by the person using the service as the desired response to their assessed need.
- Keep it simple. Do not make unrealistic demands on participants. Good research starts with specific and answerable questions.

Note the need to provide written definitions of what you are aiming to do and how you will measure that it has been achieved. The possibilities of projects that improve services can be endless. They could include:

- Various forms of groupwork, such as support and mutual help groups;
- Ways of addressing specific service user needs – young people involved in or affected by violence, older people experiencing isolation and loneliness;
- Community projects undertaken jointly with other professionals such as youth and community workers;
- Developing a theory-based intervention approach for specific service user groups;
- etc.

Some projects will involve working together on areas of service delivery that will not require additional funding. However, there may be projects for which you have to make a funding application.

Grant applications

We have already noted that you need to develop skills to research the availability of sources of funding, particularly concerning your service user group. Although these activities are beyond the remit of this book they have implications for writing, since it is important that you prepare grant applications addressing the purpose and rationale of the funder. Making grant applications involves the following.

Covering letter

As with those applying for funding for service users, the covering letter should appear professional and be reader-friendly. It introduces you and represents your initial approach to an organization. The traditional three parts state:

1. The purpose of your letter.
2. A brief outline of what the funding is for, without duplicating what is in the application.
3. What action you expect the recipient to take in response.

Executive summary

This helps those considering the application to quickly understand what you are applying for. Comprehensive yet succinct, this summary could be a couple of sentences, certainly no longer than one page. In addition to the covering letter, this introduces as well as summarizes the proposal. If it is professionally presented but easy to read it will encourage the reader to go further. It should explain the purpose of your organization and why you are making an application, but also show how the proposal is in keeping with the mission of the body to whom you are applying.

Project rationale

This is the heart of your proposal. Your aim here is to persuade the reader that what you propose to do is significant and essential and that your team or agency is the appropriate one to do it. It is best to write as if the reader does not know the issue or subject. Do not assume knowledge on the part of those considering your proposal. Explain why it is important and make a case for what you are aiming to do. Summarize any research that you have undertaken and provide evidence to support your proposal.

The project rationale may have as part of it or in separate subsections a 'need statement' and 'aims and objectives'.

Need statement

It is good to include data identifying shortfalls and case studies, stories or examples painting a picture of how the funding will help alleviate need. This should be in keeping with the interests of the body you have applied to. Your aim is to persuade the funder that what you are proposing solves a social problem and that their organization should be interested in supporting it.

Aims and objectives

These should be clearly outlined, argued and supported by evidence. You are explaining what your team or agency wants to do about the subject or issues. State what you ultimately hope to achieve, outlining specific results you expect to accomplish. Aims can be fairly broad and general. Objectives, however, are more specific and likely to lead you to outcomes and outputs.

Outcomes and outputs

Outcomes and outputs should be specific, well articulated and measurable. You can outline ways in which your goals and objectives will be SMART (specific, measurable, attainable, realistic and time limited). Funders like to have a timescale within which you will be able to inform them of results and outputs.

Methods, strategies or programme outline

It is helpful to outline in a detailed and logical way how you will achieve the aims and objectives earlier stated. You can paint a picture of how the proposed programme will unravel and take place. This section should be as precise as possible, so can include a chart listing key elements, inputs, activities, who will do what, measures and impacts. A timeline can clearly outline when activities will take place and when outcomes are expected to be achieved.

Evaluation

How will you measure whether the aims and objectives have been achieved? Funders usually prefer to be associated with a successful project. It is helpful to make clear how the impact of the project will be evaluated. Evaluation might be ongoing with records kept and data collected as well as ultimate outcome and output measures. Evaluation may cost money, particularly if there is to be some external input into research and an objective assessment of the project.

Budgeting

You need to include costings, expenses and income, if any, in as much detail as possible. It is important to make clear whether you are applying for total funding or whether you have income or funds from other sources. Some funders may prefer not to be the sole source of financial support for a project. Your agency may be contributing money or support in-kind through resources such as staffing, premises or equipment. These should be mentioned.

The timescale of the project has implications for funding. Is there a pilot stage? Is it a project that will extend into the future? Are the funds you are applying for to cover a certain period of time? It is important to outline the sustainability of a project over time.

Other Information

It can be helpful to list personnel involved, and their expertise and experience of running similar projects or related activities. It is also important to give information about your team and agency. Outline why it is appropriate for you to run the proposed project and why the funders should have confidence in you to run it effectively and use funds responsibly. The mission statement of your organization or a brief rationale for its existence can add weight to the application. State whether you are running or have run similar projects before. Again, do not assume that the funder knows your agency. Write as if to someone who does not know it.

Summary

This chapter has introduced a particular type of writing that you are likely to come across in some form as a social worker – making a case to convince others to fund an aspect of your work. While skills discussed in previous chapters apply to funding applications as well, this chapter proposed that a particular characteristic of this type of writing is persuasion – seeking to persuade someone that they should commit funds to your proposal. The chapter explored ways to put forward a reasoned and persuasive argument so that a panel or those responsible for allocating funds will be persuaded that what you are suggesting is desirable and meets their funding criteria.

The chapter considered what is involved in seeking funding within your agency, typically through applying to a panel, and in obtaining external funds for service users from charities or grant-awarding trusts. Following a brief discussion of the possibility of involvement in service development, research and evaluation projects, the chapter explored applications for funding grants.

Key points

- Professional writing skills are relevant to funding applications with the added characteristic of the use of persuasion in writing.
- To seek funding within your agency's budget you need to present a well-argued case in writing and in person, usually to a panel.
- Writing applications effectively can help you obtain additional funds for service users from charities and grant-making trusts.
- Paying attention to writing funding applications can support service development, research and evaluation projects.

Further reading

Eastwood, M. and Norton, M. (2010) *Writing Better Fundraising Applications: A Practical Guide*, 4th edition, London: Directory of Social Change.
One Westminster (n.d.) *Online Advice: How to Write a Good Funding Application*, London: One Westminster. Available at: www.onewestminster.org.uk/sites/default/files/documents/finding_grants_1.pdf.

10 Conclusion and continuing professional development

Chapter overview

By the end of this chapter you should have an understanding of:

- your own writing skills;
- your assessment of your strengths and weaknesses in writing;
- ways suggested within this book to enhance your professional writing skills;
- the aims of this book and how to develop and add to the skills outlined within it;
- pursuing your CPD in relation to professional writing.

Revisiting writing skills

At the end of Chapter 1 you will have noted, and ideally completed, a checklist of writing skills. Having now read through this book, or perhaps focused on some sections that you found most helpful, it would be good for you to revisit the checklist, reflect on your initial reaction to it and score yourself again against the variety of skills listed.

Reflection

- What was your first reaction to the writing skills checklist when you initially read through it?
- How did you feel about the number and assortment of skills listed? Surprised, overwhelmed, reassured?
- Did you recognize and relate to all or to the majority of the skills as ones that are necessary for professional writing in social work?
- How many were skills that you had not previously considered or that you thought you needed to develop?

You might have initially been taken aback by the number and variety of skills listed. You may have found it difficult to score yourself if you were not sure what some of the skills were or what they involved. On the other hand, the list might have confirmed that you had all or most of the skills to enable you to write to an expected professional level.

Review of previous chapters

The checklist anticipated a number of chapters that clarified the skills, expanded on them, suggested how they related to professional writing generally and applied them to professional writing within social work practice. Prior to the checklist Chapter 1 reflected on the debate about entry standards required before starting social work education and training, and on the level of literacy and other capabilities expected of professional social workers. The chapter put forward the view that writing matters significantly in social work for credibility as a profession. Chapter 1 also acknowledged the perception of many social workers that paperwork in recent years has increased and that it gets in the way of personal interaction with service users. While accepting that being tied up in bureaucracy and being expected to take on a heavy volume of unnecessary writing need challenging, the chapter stressed that professional writing is an essential and indispensable part of social work. Some of the skills later put forward, such as planning and making time to write, writing as an aid to thinking analytically, and expressing your professional voice in writing, were suggested as a way of integrating writing into your workload and enhancing your professionalism.

Writing can be part of your thinking. Although you will approach writing in your own individual style, managing your workload in a professional way includes preparing to write, planning and organizing your writing. These ideas were explored in Chapter 2. The chapter also outlined ways in which academic writing for university is different from professional writing, with a different audience, purpose, style, structure and acceptable standard. Writing that may just achieve an academic pass mark at university will almost certainly not reach a satisfactory professional level within a social work agency. Chapter 2 suggested skills and techniques involved in gathering information, adjusting your writing to your audience, ways of writing in plain and clear English, and structuring your writing.

Writing in a professional style and finding your professional voice are characteristics that develop with experience and confidence. Chapter 3 explored appropriate language and a professional vocabulary, including making sure that you are familiar with the meaning and spelling of words. The chapter suggested that a professional style is achieved through precise vocabulary, formal language and non-emotive expression. It also put forward ways of achieving a professional tone, including anti-oppressive language, as an important way of conveying an acceptable, value-based approach through language.

The technical aspects of writing involved in using correct grammar, punctuation and paying attention to the structural rules of language may seem to many uninteresting and one of the less exciting facets of writing. Nevertheless, attention to grammar and structure are essential for getting your message across clearly and for writing persuasively. Chapter 4 reviewed these, giving suggestions and advice, and suggesting techniques that can make your writing more robust and are essential for successful professional practice. If after reading this book you still feel that there are some gaps in your use of English, do look up the grammar books and websites that were recommended in the earlier chapters of this book.

The first four chapters, Part 1 of the book, provided an overview of professional writing. Part 2 has addressed the needs of social work practice in relation to professional writing. It applied the content of Part 1 to practice, starting with an exploration of critical analysis in professional writing. Chapter 5 returned to the idea of writing as part of thinking and suggested ways in which writing helps professionals to think analytically. Social work assessment, planning, intervention, review and evaluation form a process that is rarely simple or straightforward, therefore analytical writing is useful to help you understand how and why things happen as they do. Critical analysis through writing is a way in which social workers can play a vital role in helping other professionals to reach complex decisions. The chapter stressed that it is important to be aware of your own assumptions and to check your reasoning to ensure it is not dependent on personal assumptions. A key point of the chapter was that although there may be constraints on what social workers can write, it is important to fully develop and use your professional voice in writing.

Writing is used to communicate and 'correspond' with service users, colleagues and other professionals. Chapter 6 stressed the need to approach all correspondence in a professional manner. It is not uncommon to see emails from social work students or qualified practitioners that disregard the rules of formal writing and include lower case, abbreviations and a casual approach to writing. The chapter pointed out that, like letters and memos, emails are an official form of communication and must be formal and precise. The use of text messages in work situations is increasing in popularity and these may be somewhat more informal and flexible but must not cross professional boundaries. The chapter also explored implications relating to the growing use of social media profiles. It stressed that, as part of an increasing use of technology, social workers need to think and act ethically and pay attention to digital safeguarding. The chapter encouraged you to use the most appropriate type of correspondence for different situations and service users. It also suggested you should be aware of the legal and ethical considerations concerning all forms of correspondence.

The previously mentioned perception that paperwork in social work has mushroomed and gets in the way of personal interaction with service users is often brought up when considering the need for social workers to maintain a written record of their work. Chapter 7 reinforced the view that you should regard record-keeping as important and an essential part of social work practice. The chapter stressed the need to bear in mind the varied audiences for your records and why you are writing them – their purpose. Key points from the chapter included the need to develop your skills in writing records to a professional standard, the ability to write records as factual summaries of work undertaken and to justify professional judgements. It reminded you that when you write a record of contact with a service user you are making a note of the purpose of the interaction, and its outcome. Legislation entitles service users to see their records and gives them rights in keeping with professional social work values. The chapter suggested that it is helpful to adjust your writing style to different types of records.

Reports are a core feature of social work, used in a variety of situations from court reports to care assessments. Chapter 8 stressed the importance of structure and style in professional reports and explored how to describe, analyse and evaluate information in a report. The chapter included a reminder that, as with records, you must assess your audience and address it appropriately by adjusting your writing style to the audiences involved in reading the different types of report commonly used in social work. Reports need structure, and they require analytical thinking and writing. The need to edit them is important and this is often part of the formal supervision process, which may include legal experts who can provide expertise on matters relating to the law. It is important to remember that reports are usually required for the most complex areas of social work, so they are documents that tell the reader *why* actions were taken as well as what happened.

Your writing may sometimes involve seeking funding for aspects of your work. Applying for funding for service users may be arguably a growing need in times of austerity. Previously outlined professional writing skills are also relevant to funding applications, with an added particular emphasis on the skill of using persuasion. Chapter 9 reviewed implications for writing to obtain funding from your agency, typically a panel. It also explored effective ways of applying for additional funds for service users, usually from charities and trusts, and writing funding applications for specific projects or for research. The chapter stressed the importance of presenting a well-argued case and of being clear when outlining the background information that helps you reach the conclusion that you put forward. It is important, yet again, to know and address your audience. How applications are worded can make all the difference to their success.

This chapter brings the book to a conclusion by summarizing its content but it is not intended to suggest that we have arrived at a final destination. Coming to the end of the book can be the beginning of pursuing ways to develop and add to the skills outlined within it. The book may have highlighted skills that you already demonstrate and introduced you to new ones, but you need to continue reviewing them, be appropriately self-critical and seek feedback from others about your skills.

Seeking feedback on your writing

When you are a student on your practice placements a practice educator and, if you have one, an on-site supervisor will give you feedback on the writing that you are required to undertake for your placement agency. You can also seek feedback from team colleagues. When you are a newly qualified social worker, particularly on your ASYE, it is likely that your team manager or a senior practitioner will read your reports to monitor them. There is no reason why you may not seek feedback on different types of writing from other colleagues. Even as you gain experience and progress in your professional career there should never come a time when you are entirely self-sufficient and feel that you have no need to show some of your writing to someone else and ask them for feedback; even the most experienced professionals sometimes benefit from having another pair of eyes look at their writing.

There is a sense in which your writing can last forever. Files are kept for years and even emails can be downloaded for specific purposes after considerable periods of time. While your writing style and professional voice will strengthen and develop you should ensure that your writing can stand the test of time and that you, or others, will not be embarrassed to see what you wrote and how you wrote it after a number of years.

Those of us for whom English is not our first language may find professional writing a challenge, even years after living and working in a predominantly English-speaking country. If this applies to you, it might help you to take note of suggestions included earlier in this book and apply them to your particular circumstances. These include:

- becoming as familiar as you can with grammar and the technical aspects of writing outlined in Chapter 4;
- expanding your vocabulary, noting and learning unfamiliar words as you come across them;
- reading well-written books and articles, not necessarily about social work;
- always carefully editing your work and seeking feedback from others.

Previous chapters suggest these and many other ways in which you can enhance your professional writing skills and develop your capability in relation to specific writing tasks, whatever your native tongue and educational background. In general, the actions in the list below will help you write effectively.

Key actions for effective writing

- Accept that writing is an essential part of social work practice.
- Find ways of integrating writing into your time and workload management.
- Practise and persevere developing your writing style and finding your professional voice.
- Be creative rather than getting into a rut by using the same phrases over and over again, repeating forms of words and jargon.
- Think afresh ways of recording and putting over information.
- Be aware of your audiences and of the writing style that will be most appropriate for them – service users, colleagues, other professionals, court judges, etc.
- Adopt the point of view of the reader, rather than yours.
- Ensure you produce evidence to support your professional judgements and clearly set out reasons for your conclusions.
- When necessary and appropriate find time to write drafts that you can revise and edit.
- Use online resources and computer program facilities to correct your grammar and spelling (but beware of American spellings built into some of them and remember that none are infallible).
- Consider putting important writing aside for a few minutes, hours or a day (whether a long report or a short email) and then go back to it and look at it afresh.
- Avoid the clutter of long sentences and paragraphs. Build space into your writing to make it look attractive and reader-friendly.

- Be concise, writing relevantly and to the point, avoiding unnecessary padding.
- Use headings, subheadings and bullet points when appropriate.
- Read your writing out loud to experience the sound of it (although this may not be advisable in an open-plan office!).
- Seek feedback from others.

Reflection

- Using the above bullet points as a checklist, which actions would you say you already undertake well and make part of your professional practice?
- Which ones do you feel you could develop further?
- In what ways can you pursue these areas for development? Making an action plan for them might help you.
- Do you need to go back to sections of the book to explore further what is involved in these actions?

Continuing professional development

Writing is important for your own CPD and professional identity. CPD can involve formal and informal activities. Your employer has a responsibility to promote CPD through induction and the ASYE, or its equivalent in UK countries other than England, and by enabling training and development opportunities. Some large organizations and local authorities are able to organize a substantial programme of in-service training. Others fund employees to attend external training courses. Some do both. There may be training opportunities of this type that are related to forms of professional writing.

As part of ASYE you will be required to compile a portfolio that incorporates reflective and analytical writing. It will include critical reflection on the development of your progress as a professional at various points, how you have progressed in professional decision-making, including demonstrating reasoned judgement in relation to a practice decision, and ways in which your professional development over the course of the ASYE impacted on your professional skills, practice and outcomes. You will also have to include anonymized samples of written work that you have to undertake for your employing agency. You will no doubt agree that the skills explored in this book are relevant to all these aspects of writing.

As a professional, you must also accept responsibility for your own CPD by keeping yourself informed of training courses available and applying to attend relevant ones. You can also more informally engage in activities that will enhance your professional development. Reading is one way of doing this. You can read literature and other sources such as online sites about and related to professional writing. There are suggestions to undertake further reading at the end of each chapter in this book.

Part of pursuing your CPD can involve you in reading as widely as possible, including professional journals and the work-related writing of colleagues. You would benefit from reading about specific topics but you can also read critically the writing of other people, noting structure, style and many other factors covered in chapters of this book. You will learn from the high-quality writing of others and you may also notice not so good aspects of writing that you will want to avoid. You can keep a notebook, in a traditional way or electronically, of your or others' writing mistakes and slip-ups, and of learning points.

In England, SWE have online facilities to record your CPD, as do other regulators. Interestingly, SWE provide a choice of recording your CPD using a structured or an unstructured form. An unstructured entry may be more relevant to experiences and activities such as the above, for which you take a personal initiative. CPD is not just about training courses and formal events. The structured form enables you to enter a date, name an event, state your role in it and what you did. Entries relating to how the CPD you are recording improved your practice include questions about use of research, theories and frameworks, reflecting on your own values and their impact on your practice, how you know that the changes that you have made to your practice because of feedback have had a positive impact, the role of supervision, and the impact on the quality of your practice. Entries in the unstructured form are fewer and allow you more scope to comment generally about the quality of your practice in relation to the CPD example you are recording, and selecting the professional standards that apply to it.

Keeping a record of your CPD is how you demonstrate that you are eligible to renew your registration each year with your regulator. SWE do not specify an amount of CPD that you should undertake, so it is up to you to decide how much you need to do, taking into account your individual circumstances and how you are practising at the time. Their requirement is that, as their renewal cycle is annual, you must record some CPD every year. Their recommendation is that recording CPD at least once a quarter is good practice. These expectations may well generate a fear factor in social workers. You may wonder how you are going to cope with doing enough CPD and recording it. Since CPD involves the reflection and learning that you undertake throughout your career, it is likely to be a daily experience not, as stated above, merely involving attendance at formal training events. A significant supervision session, seeking and receiving meaningful feedback about an aspect of your writing, and showing learning from the writing of others, both colleagues' work writing and high-quality writing in books and online, could be CPD activities that you can draw upon.

Other forms of writing will also be involved in your ongoing career development. This may be in the form of preparing material for regular appraisals of your work, to reflect on a project and report back to managers, to apply for promotion, to present a paper at a professional conference, and in many other ways.

Professional Identity

You are probably currently at a particular point in your journey towards acquiring, developing and cementing a professional social work identity. You may be a social care worker, social work student, newly qualified social worker, or further on in the development of your professional career. The PCF is a holistic concept of domains that enable you to show evidence of your competence as you progress through your career. Aspects such as professionalism and being aware of and working with the profession's values and ethics help you develop your professional identity. Wenger (2000) suggests that working for an organization is not enough to constitute identity. He has put forward the idea that we can belong to communities of practice and networks. These provide us with experiences as professionals to learn and take knowledge further, our own and that of others, as we interact with varying situations and people. This book argues that writing is part of this process and development, and our professional identity in turn informs our writing. The four areas which Wenger identifies within his model are practice, meaning, identity and community.

- As an integral and integrated part of practice, writing is an active element within social work.
- Through writing social workers make meaning and create understandings of complex situations.
- Professional writing develops over time and through this process you can build your professional voice and identity.
- Professional writing represents us as a community and builds a sense of belonging to a professional community of social workers.

Developing your professional writing skills in social work can contribute to you becoming a more effective and rounded professional. Whether your writing is part of the essential requirement to undertake your work or for your own development, it will entail gathering evidence for your arguments and conclusions and presenting your thoughts in an ordered way, bringing clarity to complex situations. An aim of this book has been to outline skills so that writing becomes an indispensable part of your professional practice and gives you a sense that you have accomplished your work goals. Enjoy your writing.

Further reading

Bolton, G. with Delderfield, R. (2018) *Reflective Practice: Writing and Professional Development*, 5th edition, London: Sage.

Appendix

Answers for activities in Chapter 2

Activity 2.1 suggested answer

- X is caring for her husband who has dementia.
- There have been a number of occasions when X's husband has left the house without telling her. On one such occasion he got lost and was brought back by the police. He also left the residential home that he was staying in when X was on respite holiday.
- A genogram has been done with X.
- X has a poor relationship with her husband due to his alcohol dependency.
- X does not have much contact with her step-daughter, but she has good support from her son.

Activity 2.2 suggested answer

- How did you fall?
- Why did you fall?
- How were you feeling before you fell?
- How do you feel now?
- Was the accident avoidable or preventable?
- Is it likely to occur again?
- What adaptations can be made to the bathroom to make it safer?
- What support is already in place?
- What if any legal requirements are there?
- Which other professionals know or need to know?

Activity 2.3 suggested alternatives

Social work jargon	Suggested alternative
Carer's stress	The carer is tired, feels drained, exhausted, etc.
Community care	Services and support provided at home
Multi-agency approach	An approach which is negotiated by a number of different organizations or agencies
Person-centred approach	Approach based on your individual needs, identified by you
Respite care	A short break from normal caring arrangements
Service user empowerment	Building the confidence and independence of service users
Value-driven policy	Policy which is based on a set of professional values

Activity 2.4 alternatives

- CHIN – child in need.
- Integrated care – a comprehensive, multidisciplinary approach to care (particularly between health and social services).
- LSCB – local safeguarding children board.
- Ongoing – continuing/in progress.
- Personalization – taking into account individual needs, choice and control.
- Pre-assessment – identification of issues/conditions before a formal assessment is carried out (often undertaken with a pre-assessment checklist).
- Psychosocial support – support which considers the individual's psychological state and their social environment.
- Reablement – supporting people to regain the ability to look after themselves after an illness or injury.
- Resource allocation system (RAS) – a system used to explain to individuals what resources are available to them.
- Sect. 47 – Section of the Children Act 1989 placing a duty on local authorities to investigate circumstances of children at risk of significant harm.
- Significant harm – the threshold criteria in the Children Act 1989 that justifies compulsory intervention in family life in the best interests of children.
- Wellbeing – positive mental and physical condition of an individual.

Activity 2.5 suggested answer

The Mental Capacity Act 2005 contains five principles:

1. You have presumed capacity.
2. You have all the support you need to make a decision.
3. If you make an unwise decision, this does not indicate that you do not have the capacity to understand.
4. If you are deemed to be lacking capacity, then a 'best interest meeting' takes place (this acts on your behalf).
5. In order to respect your basic rights and freedom, we put in place the least restrictive option.

We must ensure that you can retain, evaluate and communicate information with regards to the decision before we judge your capacity.

Activity 2.6 suggested changes

Home visit: Private fostering assessment. 04/03/20XX (T is privately fostering D).
Aim: To find out more about T and her family set-up.
Method: Genogram.
Findings: Although T has experienced hardships in her own life, she is positive that she can provide care for a foster child. T has conflict with her older children because she feels that they do not contribute to the family through domestic work or paid employment. These children have now left home. T's mother assisted the children to leave and T bears resentment towards her mother because of her role in this.
Conclusion: Further assessment is necessary, appointment made for 14.03.20XX.

Answers for activities in Chapter 3

Activity 3.1 suggested changes

*X suggested she was unmotivated to attend the Alcoholics Anonymous group;
however, she has done other activities such as: joined a local walking group,
attended a parenting group and avoided drinking alcohol. This has been a positive experience and she is determined to maintain these habits. She has tried
without success to contact the children's school. She is not sure how to proceed so
we discussed options and agreed an action plan.*

Activity 3.2 suggested answer

1. The effects of the right to buy policy are still being felt today. (**correct**)
2. If the school applies this **principal** strictly, children with behavioural problems will be excluded from school much more often. (**incorrect – principle**)
3. The social worker has been practising their profession for the past 15 years
   (**correct**).
4. There is no need to prove **you're** ID in school. (**incorrect – your**)
5. **There** children have been living in care for three and a half months. (**incorrect – their**)

Activity 3.4

Your notes might include:

- 7 years old/good physical health/poor coordination and fine motor skills.
- ADHD/ASD – medication – mixed results.
- Speech well developed.
- Difficulty regulating emotions especially at school – excluded twice.

Suggested summary:

*X is 7 years old and in good physical health, but his fine motor skills and coor-
dination are lower than an average child of this age. X has been diagnosed with
ADHD and ASD for which he is on medication. This has had mixed results. X
has well-developed speech and a wide vocabulary which makes him seem mature,
but he has difficulty regulating his emotions, especially at school. This causes
difficulties and he has been formally excluded twice from school.*

The example summary has distilled the information given in the initial assessment report into four sentences which focus on the facts of the case and the information which other professionals would need to know if they were to begin to
work with this child.

Activity 3.5 suggested answers

1. It is **likely that many** looked-after children do not have a positive experience
   of education.
2. Good parenting does not occur for **some** children.

3. This **indicates** that children are . . .
4. This policy **can make** survivors of domestic abuse feel isolated.
5. Disabled people **have fewer qualifications** in comparison to **the general population.**
6. X **lacks confidence** which **can** make her dependent on her father.

Activity 3.6 suggested answer

X has a disability which impacts on her daily living skills. She has been diagnosed with a brain tumour which has caused deterioration of her mobility; she currently uses a wheelchair and she has a diagnosis of incontinence.

Answers for activities in Chapter 4

Activity 4.1 suggested answers

Correct sentence	Why?
Recently, new evidence relating to this case <u>has emerged</u>.	The evidence emerged in the recent past and has relevance now.
Yesterday the impact of the care order <u>became</u> obvious.	The impact was obvious yesterday which is a completed action.
Since the Munro Report, various other cases <u>have reached</u> the media.	The Munro report was written in the past but other cases have current relevance.
In the last few years, people <u>have started</u> to question this approach.	The questioning started in the recent past and is still continuing.
Last year no one <u>realized</u> the importance of this development.	The development happened in the past and is complete.

Activity 4.2 suggested answers

1. It was clear that the family <u>could not continue</u> to function like this. (**This is fine**)
2. Once the police <u>had analysed</u> all of the evidence, they decided not to take matters any further. (**The analysis came before the decision**)
3. The AA group was a new experience for her because <u>she had not belonged</u> to a support group before. (**This is fine**)
4. He talked about experiences in his childhood that <u>impact</u> on his life now. (**The experiences in his childhood are complete but the impact is a current truth**)
5. After the family <u>had come</u> to terms with the truth, they were able to rebuild their lives slowly. (**Coming to terms with the truth happened before the family could start to rebuild their lives**)

Activity 4.3 suggested answers

1. Self-esteem and confidence <u>are</u> important for children's development. (**Self-esteem and confidence are two separate items**)

2. My collection of papers <u>is</u> hidden under the bed. **(The collection is one item)**
3. The couple <u>is</u> receiving relationship counselling in an effort to save their relationship. **(The couple is one item)**
4. Alcoholism and poverty <u>have</u> contributed to his breakdown. (**Alcoholism and poverty are two separate items**)
5. A small group of young people <u>was</u> seen at the scene of the crime. **(The group is one item)**

Activity 4.4 suggested answers

1. The <u>construction</u> of a new centre will be dedicated to pupils with behavioural problems.
2. The judge questioned the <u>relevance</u> of some of the evidence given by police.
3. Community groups greeted the announcement with <u>satisfaction</u>.
4. There has been an <u>improvement</u> in the council's provision of social housing in recent years.

Activity 4.5 suggested answer

On 17 January 20XX, having failed to report to the police station, X was caught on CCTV camera shoplifting food. In a statement given later that day X said, 'I was hungry and I didn't have any money, so I had to get something to eat.' Although this is a breach of X's bail order, it is the first time that something like this has happened, and he has shown immediate remorse. There is also evidence of significant improvement in his behaviour at school, home and with friends.

Activity 4.6 suggested answers

1. There are some wonderful towns to visit in Kent such as: Canterbury with its ancient Cathedral; Whitstable, famous for oysters and Dover, known throughout the world for its white cliffs.
2. The attendees at today's meeting included: Mr Bentley, PCS; Mrs Fry, head teacher; and Janet Patel, senior social worker.
3. All the way home he complained of a headache; he had been hit on the head by a football during the match at school.
4. It is easier to support a family who have volunteered for the programme; they have often discussed many of the issues which can cause conflict.
5. Nobody at the child's school had seen him for over a week; this is often the case in these situations.

Activity 4.7 suggested answers

1. The impact of lack of exercise on <u>children's</u> weight is evident in growing levels of obesity.
2. <u>Apple's</u> latest iPhone has become the most commonly stolen item in schools.
3. <u>Teenagers'</u> behaviour is influenced by their peers.
4. <u>I've</u> always preferred <u>cheese and onion</u> crisps to other flavours.
5. The role of art is to challenge <u>people's</u> ideas rather than to paint pretty pictures.

Activity 4.8 suggested answers

1. The CQC's inspection took place last week so the office was in disarray.
2. Baby P's case marked a watershed in social work practice.
3. Munro's recommendations have had far-reaching implications.
4. The social work profession has changed beyond recognition from what it was in the 1970s.
5. Elderly people in their 80s and 90s are now expected to manage their own care.

Activity 4.9 suggested answers

1. Sex education has been successful in the sense that rates of teenage pregnancy in the UK have fallen.
2. Sure Start failed in that the people accessing it were not the most in need.
3. The Munro report was useful to the extent that it highlighted shortcomings in inter-agency working.
4. The outcome for these children is positive insofar as they have been placed in long-term foster care.
5. Provision of physiotherapy for elderly people is cost-effective in that it can extend their ability to live independently.

Activity 4.10 suggested answer

*Some aspects of my first year as a social worker working in the leaving care team have been positive. **For example,** initially I was given a caseload of eight children. This gave me a chance to find information out about those children, **such as** their interests, their situations, their career or further education plans. I enjoyed this experience and felt that I was doing a good job. This was **illustrated by** positive feedback from my supervisor. **However,** since Christmas my caseload has doubled, and I have not had time for weekly supervision. This has caused me some stress and anxiety. **An example** of this is that I don't know the children as well and I am unable to give them the person-centred service that they require.*

Answers for activities in Chapter 6

Activity 6.1 suggestion for a more professional version of the email

Email
From: Edward Swales
To: Mary Attah
Subject: Message from Robert Smith

Dear Mary

Robert Smith telephoned asking for you urgently while I was on Duty. Mr Smith said his foster son (name) went missing on Saturday (insert date). They reported him missing to the police on (date) at (time). Mr Smith is wondering about implications as the LAC review is today. He wondered whether he might be able to talk to you personally and I said I would ask you to return his call as soon as you can.

Ed Swales
Student Social Worker
Fostering Team

Activity 6.2 suggested improvement for the letter

Anytown Social Services
Address

9 May 20XX
Mrs Ada Riley
28 The Avenue
Anytown
Postcode

Dear Mrs Riley

Appointment for Monday 19 May 20XX at 3pm

I write to let you know that I can come to see you on Monday 19 May at 3:00 pm.

The visit will be to make an assessment of how you are managing and whether we can help you by providing services. It will help me to see information such as recent doctor's appointments and details of your benefits and living expenses if you have these available.

I have enclosed a leaflet about our services. Please call me if there is anything you do not understand.

Please let me know if it is OK for you to see me on Monday 19th by ringing me on 12345 678910.

Yours sincerely

Linda Holmes
Social Worker

Answers for activities in Chapter 7

Activity 7.1 suggested more professional version

Home visit to Mrs Aina Akinjide to review her care package

Visited Mrs Akinjide at her home. She was active and seemed cheerful and positive. We discussed issues including:

Care needs: her mobility seemed adequate as she showed me around.
Health: she reported no problems and has not had to visit her GP recently. She is eating well. A contractor delivers frozen meals that she can heat easily and eat at a time of her choice. She has a microwave and freezer on free loan.

Networks of support: she is a member of a local church and they maintain helpful links with her. Her daughter visits weekly. She enjoys attendance at a day centre for one afternoon session per week and would like to increase this.

Leisure/relationships: her networks of support help with this. She misses her family, particularly her husband who died two years ago. At home her cat and watching TV are pastimes from which she derives pleasure.

Activity 7.2, fact or opinion?

1. I smelled alcohol on his breath. **(Fact. Although it relies on an accurate sense of smell)**
2. He is an alcoholic. **(Opinion – it could be a medical diagnosis or someone's 'label')**
3. He attends AA meetings. **(Fact if the person has confirmed this)**
4. He told me he attends AA as regularly as he can. **(Fact)**
5. He was unsteady on his feet and he seemed drunk. **(Factual observation plus an opinion)**
6. I noticed a number of empty wine and beer bottles in the kitchen. **(Fact)**

Answers for activities in Chapter 8

Activity 8.1

1.

- The main audience for this report is a judge.
- The report will be used to make a decision about a young person's life.
- The audience will need to know what the young person's life was like and how it has changed.
- The report will be used to inform.

2.

- The main audience for this report is a housing association committee.
- The report will be used to persuade the association to invest in activities for young people on the estate.
- The audience will need to know the problems that a lack of facilities for young people on the estate cause, what facilities exist on other estates and the interests which young people on the estate have.
- The report will be used to secure funding.

3.

- The main audience for this report is the management and teaching team of a school.
- The report will be used to inform teachers about a pupil's history.
- The audience will need to know the facts of the pupil's care arrangements and the effects that this has had on him/her.

• The report will be used to help teachers to understand the issues this pupil faces and put in place measures to support his/her learning and social development.

Activity 8.3 suggested answer

X's recall of the theft was given to the police during interview on [date]. X informed the police on this occasion that he had seen the telescope in a neighbouring garden and planned to take it when it was dark. X did this, taking the telescope to his own garden. This took place between [date and date].

On the second interview X gave information which has been passed on to police in regard to the involvement of an adult male of 21 years.

X's offending behaviour has historically included thefts, handling stolen goods, assault against a person and non-domestic burglary. Over the past year X has not committed any violent crime.

Activity 8.4 suggested timeline

Age	Information
5	Known to social services for difficult behaviour
6	Suffered an extreme trauma due to domestic violence
7	Deteriorating behaviour at school, speech and language difficulties, permanently excluded from school
10	First referral order for arson at family home
11	Secure accommodation order – non-communicative, noticeable stammer when speaking with people in authority
13	Subject to care order, but living back at home and integrating into the community/ special school. Three month curfew. Regularly attends school, is motivated and better behaved at school. Stammer is much improved.

Activity 8.5 suggested answer

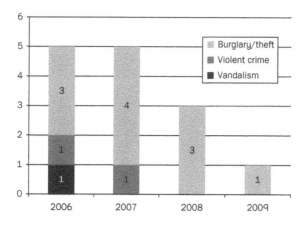

Activity 8.6 suggested answer

It is recommended that X be given a community sentence so that he can continue to make progress in his behaviour at school and at home. He is now communicating well, so it may be appropriate for him to participate in a restorative justice programme with the victim of this crime. It is also recommended that X's curfew be extended for a further three months so that he has less opportunity to commit crimes in the future and so that he starts to understand the consequences of his behaviour.

Answers for activities in Chapter 9

Activity 9.1 suggested answer

MOBILITY: Every time Mrs A walks even short distances she needs the support of two people. Her movements are quite slow and she is unsteady on her feet. Due to increased confusion she does not understand that using a walking aid can help her walk. Because of these factors Mrs A's risk of falling is high.

References

Addis, M. and Morrow, P. (2005) *Your Rights: The Liberty Guide to Human Rights*, 8th edition, London: Pluto Press. Available at: https://epdf.pub/your-rights-the-liberty-guide-to-human-rights-8th-edition.html (accessed 17 August 2020).

BASW (2018) *The Professional Capabilities Framework (PCF)*, London: British Association of Social Workers. Available at: https://www.basw.co.uk/professional-development/professional-capabilities-framework-pcf/the-pcf (accessed 18 August 2020).

BBC (2013) Essex social worker: Children put in care 'career high', *BBC NEWS Essex*, 24 May 2013. Available at: www.bbc.co.uk/news/uk-england-essex-22651876 (accessed 19 August 2020).

BDO Local Government (2012) *From Housing and Litter to Facebook and Twitter: Updating Your Status*, BDO LLP, March. Available at: www.digitalengagement.info/2012/03/20/from-housing-and-litter-to-facebook-and-twitter/ (accessed 19 August 2020).

Bishop, V. (2008) Why learn a language? The potential of additional language tuition for linguistic identity awareness and anti-discriminatory practice within British social work education, *Social Work Education: The International Journal*, 27 (8): 913–24 (accessed 7 September 2020).

Bluestein, G. (2014) Sam Olens explains a 'frustrating', explosive memo – and an opposing view, *The Atlanta Journal-Constitution*, 15 July. Available at: www.ajc.com/blog/politics/sam-olens-explains-frustrating-explosive-memo-and-opposing-view/AuxXIzxH7jO7i6ta17JqNO/ (accessed 18 August 2020).

Cooner, T.S. (2014) Using Facebook to explore the boundary issues for social workers in a networked society: Students' perceptions of learning, *British Journal of Social Work*, 44 (4): 1063–80.

Cottrell, S. (2003) *The Study Skills Handbook*, 2nd edition, Basingstoke: Palgrave.

Croisdale-Appleby, D. (2014) *Re-visioning Social Work Education: An Independent Review*, London: Department of Health. Available at: www.gov.uk/government/uploads/system/uploads/attachment_data/file/285788/DCA_Accessible.pdf (accessed 11 August 2020).

Crystal, D. (2009) *Txtng: The gr8 db8*, Oxford: Oxford University Press.

DfE (2018) *Post-Qualifying Standard: Knowledge and Skills Statement for Child and Family Practitioners*, London: Department for Education. Available at: https://assets.publishing.service.gov.uk/government/uploads/system/uploads/attachment_data/file/708704/Post-qualifying_standard-KSS_for_child_and_family_practitioners.pdf (accessed 18 August 2020).

DoH (2015) *Knowledge and Skills Statement for Social Workers in Adult Services*, London: Department of Health. Available at: https://assets.publishing.service.gov.uk/government/uploads/system/uploads/attachment_data/file/411957/KSS.pdf (accessed 18 August 2020).

DoHSC (2020) *Care and Support Statutory Guidance*, London: Department of Health and Social Care. Available at: https://www.gov.uk/government/publications/care-act-statutory-guidance/care-and-support-statutory-guidance.

Douglas, A. (2017) *Making Every Word Count for Children*, London: Cafcass. Available at: https://www.cafcass.gov.uk/2017/01/26/making-every-word-count-children/ (accessed 18 August 2020).

Dugan, E. (2014) Social workers 'need more secretaries and less paperwork', *Independent*, 29 October. Available at: www.independent.co.uk/news/uk/home-news/social-workers-need-more-secretaries-and-less-paperwork-9821833.html (accessed 11 August 2020).

Dyson, L., Munby, J. and Black, L.J. (2014) 1 WLR563, (2013) Fam Law 1515, (2013) EWCA Civ 1146, (2013) 3 FCR481, (2013) WLR(D) 348. Available at: https://www.familylawweek.co.uk/site.aspx?i=ed117048 (accessed 7 September 2020).

Firmin, C. (2020) *Contextual Safeguarding and Child Protection: Rewriting the Rules*, London: Routledge.

Hammond, K. (1996) *Human Judgement and Social Policy*, Oxford: Oxford University Press.

Kolb, D. (1984) *Experiential Learning Experience as a Source of Learning and Development*, Upper Saddle River, NJ: Prentice-Hall.

Martin, R. (2013) *Teamworking Skills for Social Workers*, Maidenhead: Open University Press.

McGregor, K. (2010) Social worker struck off after poor record-keeping, *Community Care*, 5 May. Available at: www.communitycare.co.uk/2010/05/05/social-worker-struck-off-after-poor-record-keeping/#.U3uSQyh7PHg (accessed 17 August 2020).

Moffat, F. (2012) *Writing a Later Life Letter*, London: BAAF.

Munro, E. (1999) Common errors of reasoning in child protection work, *Child Abuse and Neglect*, 23 (8): 745–58.

Munro, E. (2011) *The Munro Review of Child Protection: Final Report – A Child-centred System*, Cm 8062, Norwich: The Stationery Office. Available at: https://assets.publishing.service.gov.uk/government/uploads/system/uploads/attachment_data/file/175391/Munro-Review.pdf (accessed 11 August 2020).

Narey, Sir M. (2014) *Making the Education of Social Workers Consistently Effective*, London: Department for Education. Available at: www.gov.uk/government/publications/making-the-education-of-social-workers-consistently-effective (accessed 11 August 2020).

Olah, K. (2010) *Is it Still the 'Three Rs'?* Available at: https://en.wikibooks.org/wiki/Foundations_of_Education_and_Instructional_Assessment/Curriculum/Three_R%27s (accessed 11 August 2020).

Ormiston, H. (2013) *Serious Case Review Overview Report in Respect of Child 1*, Bolton: Bolton Safeguarding Children Board. Available at: https://www.boltonsafeguardingchildren.org.uk/downloads/download/8/child-death-and-case-reviews (accessed 17 August 2020).

Pemberton, C. (2010) Danger signs that lay in a timeline: How social workers should use case chronologies, *Community Care*, 27 September. Available at: www.communitycare.co.uk/2010/09/27/danger-signs-that-lay-in-a-timeline-how-social-workers-should-use-case-chronologies/#.U4clsyh7PHg (accessed 17 August 2020).

QAA (2019) *Subject Benchmark Statement: Social Work*, London: Quality Assurance Agency for Higher Education. Available at: https://www.qaa.ac.uk/docs/qaa/subject-benchmark-statements/subject-benchmark-statement-social-work.pdf?sfvrsn=5c35c881_6 (accessed 7 September 2020).

Romaine, M., Turley, T. and Tuckey, N. (2007) *Preparing Children for Permanence*, London: BAAF.

Saleebey, D. (2012) *The Strengths Perspective in Social Work Practice*, 6th edition, Boston: Pearson Education.

SCIE (2010) *Practice Development: Collaborative Working in Social Care*, SCIE Guide 34, London: SCIE. Available at: www.scie.org.uk/publications/guides/guide34/ (accessed 14 August 2020).

Stevenson, L. (2017) Social worker sanctioned for 'clearly inappropriate' sharing of sensitive data, *Community Care*, 12 October. Available at: https://www.communitycare.co.uk/2017/10/12/social-worker-sanctioned-clearly-inappropriate-sharing-sensitive-data/ (accessed 18 August 2020).

Swales, J. and Feak, C. (2012) *Academic Writing for Graduate Students: Essential Tasks and Skills*, 3rd edition, Ann Arbor, MI: The University of Michigan Press.

SWE (2019) *Professional Standards*, Sheffield: Social Work England. Available at: www.social-workengland.org.uk/standards/professional-standards/ (accessed 18 August 2020).

SWE (2020) *Professional Standards Guidance*, Sheffield: Social Work England. Available at: www. socialworkengland.org.uk/standards/guidance-documents/professional-standards-guidance/ (accessed 18 August 2020).

SWRB (2012) *Building a Safe and Confident Future: Maintaining Momentum*, London: Social Work Reform Board. Available at: www.gov.uk/government/publications/building-a-safe-and-confident-future-maintaining-momentum-progress-report-from-the-social-work-reform-board (accessed 11 August 2020).

Unison (2014) *Social Work Watch – Inside an average day in social work*, London: Unison and Community Care. Available at: https://www.unison.org.uk/content/uploads/2014/06/TowebSocial-Work-Watch-final-report-PDF2.pdf (accessed 11 August 2020).

Unison (2016) *A Day in the Life of Social Work*, London: Unison and Community Care. Available at: https://www.unison.org.uk/content/uploads/2017/03/CC-SocialWorkWatch_report_web. pdf (accessed 11 August 2020).

Wenger, E. (2000) Communities of practice and social learning systems, *Organization*, 7 (2): 225–46.

Westwood, J. (2014) *Social Media in Social Work Education*, Northwich: Critical Publishing.

Wilkins, D. and Boahen, G. (2013) *Critical Analysis Skills for Social Workers*, Maidenhead: Open University Press.

Williams, K. (1995) *Writing Reports*, Oxford: The Oxford Centre for Staff Development.

Index

A page number in **bold** denotes the reference is in a checklist

Abbreviations
  Activity 27
  avoid 27, 101
  in text messages 88
  no, as an expectation of
    correspondence 80
  plural, and use of apostrophe 58
Abstract nouns
  avoiding **15**, 28
Academic writing
  and use of first person 25
  citing sources 36
  different from writing for professional
    practice 20–21
  vs. professional writing **15**
Access to written information by service
    users and carers
  as an aspect of professional writing 20
  as part of the objective of case notes 22
  in relation to records 24, 97, **104**
  unacceptable in relation to personal social
    media profiles 90
  under the Data Protection Act 2018 9–10,
    81, 104
Action plan(s)
  as part of the reflective learning cycle 115
  records focused on agreed, 101
  use of 107
  writing professional **17**
Active sentences/verbs
  using **15**, 25
Active voice
  in correspondence 80
  in letters 85
Activists, as an approach to writing 19
  see also Adrenaline junkies; Reflectors;
    Scaffolders
Adjective(s)
  noun form 53
  used to give emphasis in persuasive
    writing 40

Adrenaline junkies, as an approach to
    writing 19
  see also Activists; Reflectors; Scaffolders
Adverbs
  used to give emphasis in persuasive
    writing 40
Aims and objectives
  how they will be achieved in methods,
    strategies or programme outline 134
  how they will be measured in evaluation 135
  in grant applications 133–134
Analysis/Analysing/Analytical
  and intuition in practice 65
  and rhetorical approach 66
  as part of the reflective learning cycle 115
  critical 65–66, 73
  critical vs. descriptive writing 68
  discourse 23
  expressions that reflect 41
  in a report 114
  information in a report 117, **124**
  lack of, in a report 73
  language 41–42
  move from descriptive writing **78**
  popular opinion rather than 76
  right brain 77
  skills applied to persuasive writing 66
  text 23
  using words and phrases that indicate **16**
  vs. descriptive writing 68, **78**
  vs. intuitive decision making 65
  writing
    as part of reflective writing in reports 115
    logic and evidence leading to 77
Answering questions report readers may
    have **124**
Anti-oppressive language 33
  see also Non-oppressive language
Apostrophe(s)
  Activity 58
  correct use of **16**, 57

to indicate contractions 57
to indicate possession 57
Approaches to writing
  see Activists; Reflectors; Adrenaline
    Junkies; Scaffolders
Argument(s)
  'appeal to popularity' 76
    Example 76
  as part of critical writing 67, 77
  as part of robust writing techniques 58
  biased 72
  citing sources to support, in academic
    writing 36
  confusing causes with consequences 75
  emphasizing positive aspects in persuasive
    writing 39
  gathering evidence for, as part of developing
    your professional writing skills 144
  given for recommendations 74
    Example 74
  introducing examples to add weight 60
  making judgements to structure or see both
    sides 66
  paragraphs as building blocks 29
  reasoned and persuasive, in funding
    applications 126–127
  select and justify inclusion of information
    to avoid missing the point of 72
  'slippery slope' 75
    Example 75
  'straw man' 76
    Example 76
  weak 75–76
  see also Counter-arguments
Assessed and Supported Year in Employment
    (ASYE) 12, 14, 140, 142
Assessed Year in Employment (AYE)
  in Northern Ireland 12
Assessment
  contact 103
  initial 22, 69, 98
  mental health 99
  planning-intervention-review and
    evaluation process 98, 126
  report(s) 23, 118–119
    and computer templates 67
    Activity 40, 120
    reading other colleagues', to learn 33
  risk 42, 77
  summary, in application for residential care
    (Example) 129

Assumptions, see Bias
Audience(s)
  address your, in funding applications 126
  adjusting your writing to specific **15**
  assessing your **15**
  for contact or running records 106
  for records 97, 101
  for reports 113
    Activity 113
  power relations with, as part of having a
    professional voice 74
  social workers communicating with
    multiple 6
  when writing for university vs. professional
    writing 20
  who are they, what do they need to know? 24

Bias(es)
  avoiding personal, in relation to
    records 101
  check for, and assumptions 70, 71
    Example 71
  checking for, in your writing and others' **16**,
    68, 77
  emotional or emotive language exposing 42
  intuitive practice flawed by 65
  no personal, in records 101
  personal, as part of being judgemental 66
  private opinions and, on place in
    professional recording 7
  questioning 72
    Example 71
  your own, and subconscious, in reports 116
  see also Unbiased
Budgeting
  in grant applications 135
Bullet points
  using, as key action for effective writing 142
  see also List(s)
Bureaucracy/Bureaucratic
  burdens, distracting social workers 6
  in social work 96

Care plan(s)
  agreed with a service user 89
  as a writing task with objectives 22
  focus on, in record keeping **105**
  part of different purposes of professional
    writing 20
  persuasive writing for a more
    comprehensive 39

setting objectives for, with a 'mind map' 23
use of 107
writing professional **17**
Case notes, see Case records/recording or
    case notes
Case records/recording or case notes
as a writing task with objectives 22
as part of a social worker's average day 5
not keeping adequate 95
use of 105
writing professional **17**
Case review reports 118
Changing your mind
as good practice 72
Charities, see Trusts
Charts and diagrams
Activity 122
interpreting, and data **17**
using, in reports 116
Check(ing)
accuracy of all information in a report **124**
and proofread letters 84
before documents enter the public domain 30
facts retrospectively through records 98
for bias **16**, 68, 70, 72, 77
see also Editing and checking
Chronologies
containing information that needs to be
    shared 100
Example 109
use of 108
writing professional **17**
Clarity
and simplicity in writing 24
as a required skill for day and residential
    work records 106
need for 100
professional writing requires, so clear
    definitions are vital 20
Clauses
using commas to separate two
    independent 54
using semicolon to separate two
    independent 56
Client, as a term 44
see also Patient; Service user
Colloquial(isms)
to be avoided 34
Colon(s)
correct use of **16**, 55-56
used to introduce a list 56

Comma(s)
correct use of **16**
placed between the condition and the
    consequence in description 39
rules that govern the use of 54–55
    Activity 55
Computer/online templates
for memos 87
for reports, assessments 66, 73
Conclusion(s)
draws, as part of critical analytical writing 68
flow to a logical, in funding applications 129
in reports 112, 114
limit the, to avoid inflexible
    recommendations 68, 76–77
logical, in last paragraph of a letter 84
reaching 66, 67
strengthening arguments for 74
to end a life letter 86
Confidentiality
concerning emails 82
in relation to social media / technology 91, 92
integrity and, as part of GDPR 10
policies 80
Conjunctions
commas used to separate 54
to link two parts of a sentence 30
using **15**
Consolidation Programme
in Wales 12
Contact or running records
use of 106
writing professional **17**
Contexts and organizations, PCF domain 8
Continuous Professional Development (CPD)
    142–143
importance of writing for **17**
initiatives, beyond this book 14
record 12
Contraction(s)
correct use of **16**
using apostrophe for 57
Convincing
the reader 61, **78**
Correspondence
memo was not 87
professional expectations of 79–80
writing professional **16**
Counter-arguments
as part of critical thinking and writing 64
to explore weaknesses 75

Court report(s)
   as a type of progress report 119
   as a writing task with objectives 22
   criticism of a social worker's 73
   developing a professional voice in 74
Covering letter
   in grant applications 132, 133
Critical analysis
   as basis for decision making 65
   importance of 66
   lack of 73
   logic and evidence leading to 76
   words and phrases indicate it has taken
      place 41
Critical (analytical) writing
   acting as a written argument 66
   checklist for **78**
   select information that you include in 72
   six steps in 68
   vs. descriptive writing 68
   what is 67
Critical reflection and analysis, PCF domain 7
Croisdale-Appleby, Professor 6
Crossing professional boundaries
   see Professional, boundaries

Data Protection Act 1998 9
Data Protection Act 2018 9, 10, 11, 81, 83, 104
Day (and residential) work records
   use of 106
   writing professional **17**
Decision making
   analytical vs. intuitive 65
   as a purpose of reports 112
   complex and difficult 66
   critical analysis as basis for 65
   records essential for informed 98
Describing
   a process **15**, 38
   add, or additional information within a
      sentence 55
   and identifying impact **17**
   information in a report 116
      Activity 119-120
Descriptive
   detail, avoid unnecessary **105**
   detail, danger of including too much in
      records 100
   vs. critical analytical writing 68, **78**
   writing, as part of reflective writing in
      reports 108

Detail
   amount of 39
   asking the right questions 70
      Activity 70
   finding more 69
      Example 69
   unnecessary, in minutes 110
   see also Descriptive detail
Diagrams
   interpreting, (and charts and data) **17**
   using charts and 116
Digital
   data processing, addressed by legislation 9
   immigrants 88
   natives 88
   safeguarding 91, 139
Discourse analysis 23
Discrimination
   experience no, as a right for citizens 10
   minimize multiple 42
   social workers aware of, PCF requirement 24
Distributing documents, procedures for 30
Diversity, PCF domain 7
Drop down menus 102
   see also Computer templates

Editing and checking
   a report 123
   as part of approaches to writing 19
   revise, as a key action for effective
      writing 141
   see also Check(ing)
Effective writing
   key actions for 141-142
Email(s)
   Activity 82
   appropriateness 81
   can be downloaded after considerable
      periods of time 141
   etiquette 81
   in relation to distributing documents 30
   included in data protection legislation 9
   included in need to record all contact **105**, 106
   leave and then look afresh, as a key action
      for effective writing 141
   memos largely superseded by 86
   to school, as a writing task with
      objectives 22
   use of 81–83
   writing professional **16**
English not first language 12, 18, 24, 80, 141

Ethics
  included in aspects on which interpretation
      of evidence can be based 68
  included in aspects that help you develop
      professional identity 144
  professional, in relation to text messages 89
European Convention on Human Rights 11
Evaluating
  information in a report 116
  options, in a report 117
  reliability and validity of information, as
      part of critical reflection and analysis 7
Evaluation
  in grant applications 135
  positive and negative learning, as part of
      the reflective learning cycle 115
Evidence
  conflicting 66
  enough, upon which to base a decision 72
  gathering as much as you can 68
  gathering relevant, to include
      in reports **16**
  judgements based on 41, 66-67, 102, 141
  new, influencing assumptions 69
  reference to, in professional writing 21
  strong, to support recommendations
      74, **78**
  supporting critical (analytical) writing 68
  to support a proposal, as part of project
      rationale 134
  to support/build an argument 72, 76-77, 144
  to support recommendations in a report
      114, 117, 119, **124**
Examples
  adding, to strengthen your writing **16**
  introducing 58, 60
    Activity 60
Executive summary
  in grant applications 134
External sources/funds (charities, trusts)
  obtaining 130–131
  writing funding applications **17**

Facebook, 90, 91, **92-93**
  Messenger 91
  social worker dismissed due to comments
      on 90
Feedback
  being open to and accepting of 14
  learning from 30
  seeking, on your writing 140, 142

First person
  using appropriately **15**
  using in support plans 108
  using *you, we, I* 25
Flickr 90
Formal
  care plans 107
  conventions 80, 82-83, 84
  correspondence must be 79
  language 34, 87
  language and professional vocabulary 35
  structure/style for reports 117, **124**
  text messages 88
  using a noun to make writing sound more
      precise and 53
  writing style, adjusting as appropriate **15**
  writing style for university and professional
      writing 21
Free text (boxes)
  in computer templates 66
  making effective use of **17**
  opportunities, using 73
  see also, Drop down menus
Freedom of Information Act 2000 11
Funding applications
  obtaining external funds 130–132
  Example 131
  within your agency 127–130
    Examples 129, 130
  writing **17**

Gathering information
  Activity 23
  as the start of the writing process **15**, 23
General Data Protection Regulation (GDPR)
      9, 10, 80-81, 83, 104
Google **92**
Grammar
  correct, in emails 81
  of sentences 52
  structural rules of language 4
  use online resources to correct, as a key
      action for effective writing 141
Grant applications 133–134
Graph, see Charts and diagrams

Heading(s)
  and sections for care plans 107
  as part of funding requests forms 129
  as part of structure and style in
      professional reports 113

use of, as a key action for effective
    writing 142
using, (and paragraphs) to structure
    writing **17**
see also Subheadings
Human Rights Act 1998 11
Hypothetical questions/thinking
    as part of critical writing 67
    'slippery slope' move to negative
        scenario 75
    to analyse information in a report 117

Identity, professional
    see Professional identity
Impact of information
    identifying and describing 112,**17**
Informal
    blurring lines between formal and 79
    CPD involving activities that can be formal
        and 142
    some writing is deliberately 34
    style for emails, appropriateness of 82
    style for texts, appropriateness of 88
    writing style, adjusting as appropriate **15**
Information
    as part of checklist for editing and
        checking a report **124**
    committed to writing, in relation to
        confidentiality 79
    describing, analysing and evaluating, in a
        report 116–117
    facts, observations, as part of the reflective
        learning cycle 115
    finding out, as part of scaffolders'
        approach 19
    gather evidence and find detail 69
    gathering **15**, 23
        Activity 23
    implications of legislation for 9, 104
    importance of agencies sharing 19
    in relation to distributing documents 30
    in relation to instructions 38
    needed by audiences 24
    recording significant **105**
    referring to sources of, as part of writing
        for university 21
    select and justify for inclusion 68, 72
    standardized, with computer templates
        66-67, 73
    subheadings enabling readers to get
        directly to the required 30

summarizing 40
to convey, relating to purposes of
    professional writing 22
ways of recording a putting over 139
Initial assessment
    see Assessment, initial
Instagram 90
Instructions
    Activity 38
    describing a process similar to giving 38
    giving, within your writing **15**, 27, 38
    writing, to someone **15**
Intervention and skills, PCF domain 7, 96
Intuitive
    practice 65
    vs. analytical decision making 65

Jargon
    Activity 26, 27
    and formal language 35
    avoid, in care plans 106
    avoid, in correspondence 80
    avoid, in records 101, 102, **105**
    being creative instead of using, as key
        action for effective writing 141
    free report **124**
    in a funding application form 128
        Activity 129
    social work 26, 27, 124
Job applications, making an impression 4

Key sentences
    at the beginning of paragraphs 29
    inserting **15**
Knowledge, PCF domain 7
Knowledge and Skills Statements (KSS) 8, 12

Language
    adjusting, in correspondence 80
    adjusting, in letters 84
    ambiguous, in emails 83
    analytical 41
    complex, avoiding 27, 102
    derogatory or emotive, avoid in record
        keeping **105**
    formal 33, 35, 87
    hedging, when introducing a qualifying
        statement 59
    important for records 101
    in relation to text messages 88
    limit your conclusion with use of 77

non-discriminatory 42
non-discriminatory and non-oppressive,
    using **16**
objective, in academic writing style 21
pay attention to tone and, in later life
    letters 86
plain, in reports 114
streamlining 123
style, to fit the purpose of professional
    writing 22, 34
technical, use of 26
used, as part of professional identity 42
see also Anti-oppressive language; Non-
    discriminatory language; Signposting
    language
Later life letters
    content 86
    implications for other writing and
        transferable skills 86
    use of 86
    writing professional **16**
Left (analytical) brain 77
Legislation 9-11, 97, 104
    obscene publications, applicable to
        emails 83
    see also Access to written information by
        service users and carers
Letter(s)
    Activity 85
    appropriateness 80, 83–84
    content 84
    included in contact or running
        records 106
    use of 83–85
    writing professional **16**
    see also Covering letter; Later life letters
List(s) (of items)
    Activity 29
    appropriateness in academic vs.
        professional writing 21
    required punctuation in 56
    use of 'such as' for 60
    using, when appropriate in your writing
        15, 28
Logic
    and evidence supporting
        recommendations **78**
    appropriateness to arguments 76
    not assume that a reader will use the same
        as you 72
    putting forward a reasoned argument 4

Meaning
    clear, in emails 83
    give a clear, to illustrate technical language 26
    of words, being clear about **15**
    of words, Example 36–37
    of words, Vocabulary 44–46
    precise 35
    within professional identity 144
Memo(s)
    administrative management style (AMS) 87
    Example 87
    subject to formal conventions of
        correspondence 80
    use of 86–87
    writing professional **16**
Methods
    in grant applications 134–135
    part of information in a report 113
    within structure of a report 114
    see also Programme outline
Mind map(s)/mapping
    for capturing information and organizing
        your thoughts 23
    sample 24
    using, or other planning tools **15**
Minutes (of meetings)
    part of information subject to legislation 11
    part of information that needs to be shared
        100
    part of material seen during a serious case
        review 98
    use of 10-110
    writing professional **17**
Munro
    Common errors of reasoning in child
        protection work 68, 69, 70, 67, 71,
        72, 77
    Report/Review of Child Protection 6,
        19, 113

Narey, Sir Martin 4, 6
Need statement
    in grant applications 134
Neuro-linguistic programming (NLP) 23
Non-discriminatory language
    using **16**
    writing tone and 42
Non-oppressive language
    Activity 43
    using **16**
    see also Anti-oppressive language

Noun(s)
  abstract, avoid **15**, 28
  based sentences 73
  care when using a pronoun instead of a 38
  collective 52
  forms, to start sentences as part of
    academic writing style 21
  in relation to possession 57
  phrases, using **16**, 53
    Activity 54
  subject of a sentence 52

Object
  as part of a sentence 25
  subject, verb, sequence in professional
    writing style 21
Objective(s)
  clear for every writing task **15**
  Example 22
  in action plans 107
  of professional writing 22
  setting clear, with a 'mind map' 23
  see also Aims and objectives
Online social media profiles
  Activity 92-93
  application of planning to 80
  use of 90
  writing professional **16**

Opinion(s)
  differences of, to be avoided in records 97
  Informed, arriving at 66
  initial, in relation to bias and assumptions 71
  personal, appropriateness in professional
    writing 22, 102
  pieces, in newspapers 34
  popular, applicable to a type of argument 76
  private, no place in professional recording 7
  professional, in funding applications 131
  professional, in record keeping **104**
  vs. fact when describing information in a
    report 116
    Activity 102
Outcomes
  and outputs, in grant applications 134
  clear, in action plans 107
  desired, in projects and other proposals 132
  explanation of the, in case review reports 118
  goals and, in funding applications 128
  meeting learning, as part of the purpose of
    writing at university 20

Paperwork
  and social work 5
  as part of Contexts and Organizations PCF
    domain 8
  complains about 19
Paragraph(s)
  avoid long, as a key action for effective
    writing 141
  in a covering letter for grant applications 132
  in the body of a letter 84
  structuring **15**, 29
  using, (and headings) to structure writing **17**
Passive sentences
  compared with abstract nouns 28
  knowing when it is appropriate to use **15**
  use of in persuasive writing 40
  vs. active verbs and 25
Patient, as a term 44
  see also Client; Service user
People who use services, as a term 44
Persuasive writing 39
  analytical skills applied to 66
  for funding applications 126–127
  paragraphs as building blocks for 29
  writing persuasively **15**
Phrases
  explanatory, use 59-60
  noun, using **16**, 53
    Activity 54
  service user's own words and, in care
    plans 106
  shorthand, avoid in records **105**
    Activity 129
  that indicate analysis, using words and
    16, 41
  using the same, avoid, as key action for
    effective writing 141
Pinterest 90
Planning (one's writing)
  and making time to write **15**, 23
  before writing, approaches to 19
  tools, mind maps or other **15**
  your writing 18
Possession
  using apostrophe to indicate 57
Post Registration Training and Learning
  in Scotland 12
Presentation skills
  when seeking funding within your agency 127
Problem-process-solution, step by step
  account 73

Professional
  boundaries
    crossing, in relation to emails 83
    crossing, in relation to online social
      media profiles 90
    crossing, in relation to text messages 89
  correspondence, writing **16**
  identity, CPD and 13, 142
  identity, importance of writing for **17**, 42,
    142, 143-144
  judgement, in practice 41, 77, 97, 99
  judgement vs. being judgemental 66, 102
  records, writing **17**, 101
  social work values 10, 80, 97, 104, 111
  style, applying to a range of writing tasks 38
  style, writing in a **15**
  vocabulary, using **15**, 35, 44–46
  voice, developing, expressing your **16**, 74
    Activity 21
  writing vs. academic writing **15**, 20–21
Professional Capabilities Framework (PCF) 7,
  24, 99, 143, 144
Professional leadership, PCF domain 8
Professional Standards
  see SWE Professional Standards
Professionalism, PCF domain 7, 12, 18, 144
Programme outline
  in grant applications 134-135
  see also Methods
Progress reports 119
Projects
  and other proposals 132-133
  expertise in running similar 135
  writing funding applications for **17**
Pronoun(s)
  care when using 38
  first person, use of 25–26
  in subject-verb agreement 52
  to avoid repetition 35
Proofread/reading
  a report 123, **124**
  and check letters 85
  your work 61
Proposals
  and projects 132-133
  writing funding applications for **17**
Purpose(s)
  clear for every writing task **15**
  clear, within a professional voice 74
  of a letter 84
  of a meeting **104**, 110

  of data, appropriate within legislation 10
  of funding applications 131, 133
  of professional writing 22
  of records 97-100, 105-106
  of reports 112
  of writing for university vs. professional
    writing 20
  personal, emails not used for 83
  range of 33

Qualifying statement(s)
  Activity 59
  adding **16**, 59

Rs, the three ('reading, 'riting, 'rithmetic') 3
Reasoning
  as part of critical writing 67–68
  common errors of 68–69
  critical and reflective 7
  identify main line of 74
  persuasive line of, in funding applications 127
Reasons
  acceptable, for funding applications 128
  giving, in critical analytical writing 68
  giving, in reports 112, 119
  identifying, why things happen as they do **17**
  phrases which show 59
  questioning, to check for bias 71
  responding to, why a report was requested
    124
  to support conclusions, as a key action for
    effective writing 141
  within arguments 74, 77
  within later life letters 86
Recommendation(s)
  action plan, as part of the reflective
    learning cycle 115
  Activity 123
  as part of objectives for assessment and
    report 22
  avoid inflexible 76-77
  Example 39
  in reports 112, 113, 114, 117, 118–119
    Activity 116
  inflexible, avoid in critical writing 64
  making realistic **16**
  SMART 115-116
  supported with evidence 74, **78**, **124**
Record keeping, see Record(s)
Record(s)
  Activity 101

as part of evaluation within a grant
    application 135
audience for 97
Example 99, 103
keeping 89, **104-105**
maintaining to a professional standard 95–96
purpose of 97–98
social worker struck off due to poor record
    keeping 95
style of writing 100-101
subject to legislation 11, 104
to aid clear thinking 19
types of 105–108
writing professional **17**
see also Access to written information by
    service users and carers
Redundancy (in writing)
avoiding, and repetition **15**, 35
Reflective writing
as an approach 19
in reports 115
Reflectors, as an approach to writing 19
see also Activists; Adrenaline junkies;
    Scaffolders
Repetition, avoid
and redundancy **15**, 35
as part of editing and checking reports 123
in funding applications 129
Reports/report writing
Activity 119, 120, 122, 123
analytical, recommended by guidance 6
and computer templates 66
as part of a social worker's average day 5
as requirements of Intervention and Skills
    PCF domain 96
audience for 113
    Activity 113
checklist before submitting 124
complex, in relation to approaches to
    writing 19
editing, proofreading and checking 123
familiarity with different types your agency
    uses **17**
gathering evidence to include in **16**
in relation to analytical writing 72–74
learning from others' 30, 33
meeting PCF domains 7
purpose 112
reflective writing in 115–116
structure 113–114
style 114

subject to legislation 9-10
to a professional standard 112
types commonly used in social work
    118-119
within writing as part of thinking 18
Residential work records, see Day and
    residential work records
Responding/responded
directly to reasons for a report's request **124**
to emails, avoid overuse of 'Reply All' 82
Rhetoric / rhetorical
analytical and, style / skills 66, 77
using language effectively and
    persuasively 4
Right (intuitive) brain 77
Rights, justice and economic well-being, PCF
    domain 7
Risk assessment (instruments) 66
no substitute for professional judgement 77
see also, Assessment, risk
Running records, see Contact or running
    records

Safeguarding 91
addressed by chronologies
concerns must be recorded 101
improving, as the focus of a project
see also Digital safeguarding
Scaffolders, as an approach to writing 19
see also Activists; Adrenaline junkies;
    Reflectors
Semicolon(s)
correct use of **16**, 55-56
to separate items with more than one word
    in a list 54
Sentences
average, and number of words in 24
balanced, when describing a process 38-39
conditional 53
grammatical rules within 48, 52
inserting key **15**
keeping short **15**, 24, 123
long, avoid, as key action for effective
    writing 141
noun-based, in analytical writing 73
semicolon to join two independent 56
starting, with noun forms, in academic
    writing 21
upper case at the start of 80
using active **15**, 25
using passive **15**, 25

verb in agreement with subject in, ensuring **16**
see also Active sentences/verbs; Key sentences; Passive sentences
Serious case review 85, 98, 106, 108
Service user, as a term 44
see also Client; Patient
Short Message Service (SMS), see Text messages
Signposting
language, using **15**
to give direction and structure to writing 29–30
within records 98
SMART (specific, measurable, attainable, realistic, timely) goals
in care plans 107
in grant applications 134
in report recommendations 115
Social media
appropriate style in 80
use of 91, 92
see also Online social media profiles
Social Work England (SWE) 9, 143
Spelling
Activity 37
being vigilant about 61
correct, in emails 82
of words, being clear about **15**
of words, Example 36–37
poor, in employment applications 4
use online resources to correct, as key action for effective writing 141
Structuring
paragraphs **15**, 29
writing 31
Style, see Writing style; Professional style
Subheadings
Activity 31
to enhance records 101, **104**
Activity 101
to indicate separate sections 30
using **15**, 142
Subject (grammatical term)
as part of a sentence 25
verb agreement **16**, 52
Activity 52
verb, object sequence, in professional writing style 21
Summarizing / summary writing
Activity 40-41

essential elements of 40
using limited words **16**, 40
within minutes 110
Support plans
use of 108
writing professional **17**
SWE Professional Standards / Guidance 9, 91, 96

Techniques, see Writing techniques
Technology
based communication tools, in SWE Professional Standards
confidentiality applies to use of 92
ethical use of 91
growing use of 88
modern 81, 91
Templates, see Computer templates
Tense(s)
Activity 50, 51
all, used in English 49
correctly using more than one verb **16**, 50–51
using correct verb **16**, 48
Activity 50, 51
Text message(s)
appropriateness 88
Example 88
informal style 34
professional use 838–89
Short Message Service (SMS) 88
writing professional **16**
Thinking process, writing as part of 18
Third person
use in academic writing style 21
using appropriately **15**
Tone
adjusting your, on letters 84
negative, avoid in correspondence 102
of a text message 88
paying attention to, in later life letters 86
style and, within funding applications 126
writing 34, 42
writing in an appropriate **16**
see also Non-discriminatory language
Trivium (grammar, logic and rhetoric) 4
Trusts (charities)
obtaining funds from 131
writing funding applications **17**
Tumblr 90
Twitter 90, 91, **92**

Unbiased
  reports 118, 119
University writing, different to writing in
      professional practice 20-21
Unsubstantiated statements
  avoiding **78**
Upper case
  as part of formal conventions for
      correspondence 80

Values
  as part of professional identity 144
  in relation to online social media profiles 90
  of different practitioners 100
  showing professional, in correspondence 80
  see also Professional social work values
Values and ethics, PCF domain 7, 33, 42
Verb(s)
  abstract nouns formed from 28
  in agreement with the subject, ensuring **16**, 52
    Activity 52
  phrasal, avoid 34
  tenses, using correct **16**, 48–49
    Activity 50
  using active, and sentences **15**, 25
  using more than one verb tense correctly **16**
  using noun form for 53
Vocabulary
  formal language and professional 35
  precise, as part of editing, proofreading
      and checking reports 123
  using a professional **15**, 44–46
  within writing tone and non-discriminatory
      language 42
Voice
  active, in correspondence / letters 80, 85
  building your professional, and identity 144
  developing a professional 68, 139
  for effective writing 141
  professional 4
  professional, expressing your **16**
  service users' 24, 100, 108

Weakness(es)
  chronologies can highlight 108
  Exploring 75
  identifying in your writing and others' **16**
  learning from strengths and 33, 137
    Activity 116
WhatsApp 91

Words
  Activity 26, 27, 37
  analysis of 23
  and phrases that indicate analysis, using
      16, 41
  appropriate for the reader, using **15**, 26
  clear about meaning and spelling of, being **15**
  explain in, when using charts and
      diagrams 116
  linking, (conjunctions) and use of commas 54
  meaning of 3-37
  number of in an average sentence 24
  redundant, avoid as part of editing,
      proofreading and checking reports 123
  repetitive forms of, avoid, as key action for
      effective writing 141
  summarizing using limited **16**
  use of in approaches to writing 19
  using limited, to summarize 40
  using service users' own 107
  with emotional tone, avoid 42
  writing in full rather than using
      contractions 57
Writing
  approaches to 19
  as part of thinking 18
  communicating in, as part of PCF domains 7
  critical vs. descriptive 68
  key actions for effective 141-142
  precise, improved by using professional
      vocabulary 44–46
  professional vs. academic 20-21
  purpose of 22
  skills 4-6, **14–17**
  style
    Activity 34
    adjusting, (formal/informal) as
        appropriate **15**
    bureaucratic 28
    in reports 114, **124**
    general aspects of 34
    guidance on 33
  subject to legislation 9-10, 104
  tasks, range of 38-40
  techniques
    robust 58-60
    for reports 114
  tone and non-discriminatory language 42
  well, why it matters 3–4
  see also Paperwork